S0-BMV-139

The
Tibetan
Book of the
Dead

The
Tibetan
Book of the
Dead

This edition published in 2018 by Arcturus Publishing Limited
26/27 Bickels Yard, 151–153 Bermondsey Street,
London SE1 3HA

Copyright © Arcturus Holdings Limited

All rights reserved. No part of this publication may be
reproduced, stored in a retrieval system, or transmitted, in any
form or by any means, electronic, mechanical, photocopying,
recording or otherwise, without prior written permission in
accordance with the provisions of the Copyright Act 1956 (as
amended). Any person or persons who do any unauthorised
act in relation to this publication may be liable to criminal
prosecution and civil claims for damages.

AD006316UK

Printed in the UK

CONTENTS

INTRODUCTION

First published in 1927, *The Tibetan Book of the Dead* has sold over half-a-million copies and its translation into many other European languages has led to it becoming the most widely read Tibetan text in the West. The manuscript for this great work was discovered in 1919 by W. Y. Evans-Wentz immediately after the First World War at a time when there was a resurgence of interest in spiritualism and the fate of the recently deceased. Eight years later, he published it.

W. Y. EVANS-WENTZ

Walter Yeeling Wentz was born in Trenton, New Jersey in 1878. He developed an early interest in spiritualism from reading books in his father's library and while still a teenager read *Isis Unveiled and The Secret Doctrine* by Madame Blavatsky, founder of the Theosophical Society. After moving to California, Wentz joined the Theosophical Society in 1901 and enrolled at Stanford University, where he studied with William James and William Butler Yeats. After graduating from Stanford, he studied Celtic mythology and folklore at Jesus College, Oxford. He also adopted the name Evans-Wentz, adding a name from his mother's side of the family to his surname. He then embarked on a world tour, visiting Mexico, Europe and the Far East, prior to spending most of the First World War in Egypt from where he travelled to India, arriving in Darjeeling in 1919. That same year he acquired a copy of the *Bardo Thödol* which was published with his annotations and commentary in 1927 as *The Tibetan Book of the Dead*. This was followed by other translations of Tibetan texts, including *Tibetan Yoga and Secret Doctrines* (1935) and *Tibet's Great Yogī, Milarepa* (1951). Evans-Wentz returned to the USA during the Second World War and spent his remaining years in San Diego, where he died in 1965.

THE TIBETAN BOOK OF THE DEAD

In his introduction to the first edition of *The Tibetan Book of the Dead*, Evans-Wentz relates that he obtained his manuscript copy of the text early in 1919, from 'a young *lāma* of the Kargyüpta Sect of the Red Hat School attached to the Bhutia Basti Monastery, Darjeeling'. The manuscript was in 'a very ragged and worn condition' and, according to the young *lāma*, had been passed down through his family over several generations. Later that same year Evans-Wentz acquired a collection of Tibetan texts from Major W. L. Campbell, a British political officer stationed in Gangtok, the capital of Sikkim, who had purchased them while visiting Gyantse, a town in south-west Tibet. Evans-Wentz took these texts to Kazi Dawa-Samdup (1868–1922), the English teacher at the Maharaja's Boy's School in Gangtok, and the two men worked together over the next two months on an English translation.

In his preface to the first edition, Evans-Wentz describe himself as 'the mouth-piece of a Tibetan sage' and 'little more than a compiler and editor of *The Tibetan Book of the Dead*',which included his additional commentary and extensive footnotes. The text presented here is the same as that of the first edition of *The Tibetan Book of the Dead*, except that additional material has been confined to essential explanatory footnotes.

In his preface to the second edition Evans-Wentz explains the essential message of *The Tibetan Book of the Dead*, saying that 'the Art of Dying is quite as important as the Art of Living (or of Coming to Birth), of which it is the complement and summation.' He adds, 'in the Occident [i.e. the West], where the Art of Dying is little known and rarely practised, there is, contrastingly, the common unwillingness to die, which, as the *Bardo* ritual suggests, produces unfavourable results.'

THE BARDO THÖDOL *OR* BAR DO THOS GROL

Evans-Wentz's mention of 'the *Bardo* ritual' reminds us that the Tibetan text we now know as *The Tibetan Book of the Dead* had a practical rather than literary purpose. (The Tibetan term *bar do* means 'between two' or 'intermediate' and refers to the intermediate state or *bardo* between life and rebirth.) Evan-Wentz's Tibetan text is in fact one of many funerary texts known as the *Bardo Thödol* or *Bar do thos grol* (meaning 'Liberation through Hearing in the Intermediate State') which were read aloud in the presence of a dying or recently deceased person.

Tradition relates that these texts were among the 'treasures' (terma) secreted in various remote locations in eighth-century Tibet by Padmasambhava, the Lotus *Guru*, so that they could be revealed later, at the appropriate time. One of the 'treasure revealers' was Karma Lingpa, a 14th-century mystic, who discovered a cache of scriptural treasures on Gampodar Mountain. The cache included a set of funerary texts, the *Bar do thos grol*, which were passed down to subsequent generations through a lineage of teachers until Evans-Wentz made one of the texts available to a wider public with the publication of *The Tibetan Book of the Dead*.

THE INTERMEDIATE STATE OR BARDO

According to the *Bar do thos grol*, the intermediate state comprises three *Bardo*s: the *Chikhai Bardo* or '*Bardo* of the moment of death', the *Chönyid Bardo* or '*Bardo* of the experiencing of reality', and the *Sidpa Bardo* or 'Bardo of rebirth'. The deceased person's experience of these three *Bardos* as set out in *The Tibetan Book of Dead* is as follows:

Chikhai Bardo 1st stage: the Primary Clear Light seen at the moment of death. (The Clear Light arises from the direct experience of one's own essential nature; it is also referred to as the *Dharma-Kaya*, the 'Divine Body of Truth', Perfect Enlightenment or Buddhahood.) If the deceased recognizes the Clear Light at the moment of death, he becomes enlightened and is thus liberated from the cycle of death-and-rebirth. If not, he passes on to the next stage of the *Bardo*.

Chikhai Bardo 2nd stage: the Secondary Clear Light seen immediately after death. If the deceased recognizes the Clear Light, he is liberated. If not, he passes on to the next stage.

Chönyid Bardo: apparitions of the Peaceful and Wrathful deities, which are projections of the deceased's own mind. The *Chönyid Bardo* extends over 14 days and is divided into two seven-day periods. During the first seven-day period, the deceased comes face-to-face with the 42 Peaceful Deities which are said to emanate from the heart. If the deceased recognizes the Peaceful Deities as a reflection of his own mind, recognition and liberation are simultaneous. If the deceased does not recognize them, he enters the second seven-day period and comes face to face with the 58 Wrathful Deities which are said to emanate from the brain or head. If the deceased fails to recognize these for what they are, he is compelled to wander through the next *Bardo*.

Sidpa Bardo: the deceased's consciousness is now separated from the body, but its attachment to life is still such that it is like a body without substance, known as the mental- or desire-body. Driven unremittingly by the winds of *karma*, the deceased is compelled to wander the world, looking for somewhere to rest but finding nowhere. The suffering brought on by this seemingly endless wandering through the *Bardo* leads to the deceased person's consciousness looking on rebirth in one of six realms – those of the gods, demigods, humans, animals, hungry spirits, or in hell – as a means of bringing its suffering to an end.

The initial publication of *The Tibetan Book of the Dead* coincided with the resurgence of interest in spiritualism and the afterlife in the opening decades of the 20th century. The publication of this edition coincides with a similar resurgence of interest in the afterlife due, in part, to the many first-hand accounts of near-death experiences (NDEs) and out-of-body experiences (OBEs) reported in the Western media. (Readers may have noted a similarity between the bright light reported by many who have had a near-death experience and the Clear Light of the *Chikhai Bardo*.) Medical scientists too are expressing an interest – 2008 saw the launch of a three-year project that will gather evidence from hospitals in both the UK and USA which it is hoped will increase our understanding of NDEs and OBEs and thus shed further light on the nature of consciousness and the relationship between mind and body.

However, there is a considerable difference between enlightening scientific evidence and enlightenment. The former may increase our understanding of the mind; the latter occurs when we experience for ourselves the true nature of the mind. It was to this end that the text of *The Tibetan Book of the Dead* was read aloud to the dying or recently deceased so that they could attain enlightenment and thus be liberated from the suffering associated with the endless cycle of death and rebirth. Yet we don't need to wait until the very end of our life for an opportunity to attain enlightenment. We all have within us the potential to become enlightened at any point in our life. The key lies in our recognition of the true nature of the mind.

John Baldock

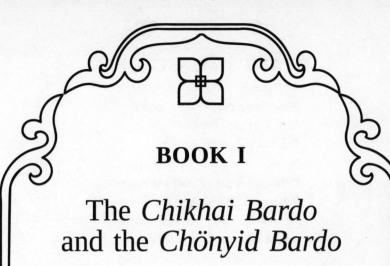

BOOK I

The *Chikhai Bardo* and the *Chönyid Bardo*

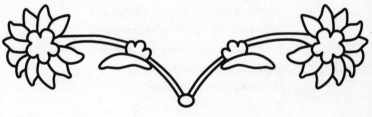

Herein lieth the setting-face-to-face to the reality in the intermediate state: the great deliverance by hearing while on the after-death plane, from 'The Profound Doctrine of the Emancipating of the Consciousness by Meditation Upon the Peaceful and Wrathful Deities'

'The *Dharma-Kāya* of thine own mind thou shalt see; and seeing That, thou shalt have seen the All – the Vision Infinite, the Round of Death and Birth and the State of Freedom.'
– Milarepa

DEATH'S MESSENGERS

All they who thoughtless are, nor heed,
What time Death's messengers appear,
Must long the pangs of suffering feel
In some base body habiting.
But all those good and holy men,
What time they see Death's messengers,
Behave not thoughtless, but give heed
To what the Noble doctrine says;
And in attachment frighted see
Of birth and death the fertile source,
And from attachment free themselves,
Thus birth and death extinguishing.
Secure and happy ones are they,
Released from all this fleeting show;
Exempted from all sin and fear,
All misery have they overcome.

Anguttara-N'kāya

THE OBEISANCES

To the Divine Body of Truth, the
   Incomprehensible, Boundless Light;
To the Divine Body of Perfect Endowment, Who
   are the Lotus and the Peaceful and the
   Wrathful Deities;
To the Lotus-born Incarnation, Padmasambhava,[1]
   Who is the Protector of all sentient beings;
   To the *Gurus*, the Three Bodies, obeisance.

---

1 Better known to Tibetans as *Guru Rinpoche*, Padmasambhava is said to have transmitted
   Tantric Buddhism to Bhutan and Tibet in the 8th century and is seen by his followers as
   the 'second Buddha'. According to tradition, he was incarnated as an eight-year-old child
   appearing in a lotus blossom.

THE INTRODUCTION

This Great Doctrine of Liberation by Hearing, which conferreth spiritual freedom on devotees of ordinary wit while in the Intermediate State, hath three divisions: the preliminaries, the subject-matter, and the conclusion.

At first, the preliminaries, *The Guide Series*,[2] for emancipating beings, should be mastered by practice.

THE TRANSFERENCE OF THE CONSCIOUSNESS-PRINCIPLE

By *The Guide*, the highest intellects ought most certainly to be liberated; but should they not be liberated, then while in the Intermediate State of the Moments of Death they should practise the Transference, which giveth automatic liberation by one's merely remembering it.

Devotees of ordinary wit ought most certainly to be freed thereby; but should they not be freed, then, while in the Intermediate State [during the experiencing] of Reality, they should persevere in the listening to this Great Doctrine of Liberation by Hearing.

Accordingly, the devotee should at first examine the symptoms of death as they gradually appear [*in his dying body*], following *Self-Liberation* [*by Observing the] Characteristics* [*of the*] *Symptoms of Death*.[3] Then, when all the symptoms of death are complete [he should] apply the Transference, which conferreth liberation[4] by merely remembering [the process].

---

2   Writings which give guidance to followers on their journey along the *Bodhi* path starting with the human world, through *Bardo*, the After-Death State, and then on to rebirth, or even *Nirvāṇa*.

3   A Tibetan work belonging to the *Bardo* cycle, often used by *lāmas* as a supplement to the *Bardo Thödol*.

4   This does not necessarily mean the achievement of *Nirvāṇa*; the liberation mentioned here is that of the 'life-flux' from the dying body in such a way that the highest level of consciousness is maintained after death, which leads to a happy rebirth.

THE READING OF THIS THÖDOL

If the Transference hath been effectually employed, there is no need to read this *Thödol*; but if the Transference hath not been effectually employed, then this *Thödol* is to be read, correctly and distinctly, near the dead body.

If there be no corpse, then the bed or the seat to which the deceased had been accustomed should be occupied [by the reader], who ought to expound the power of the Truth. Then, summoning the spirit [of the deceased], imagine it to be present there listening, and read.[5] During this time no relative or fond mate should be allowed to weep or to wail, as such is not good [for the deceased];[6] so restrain them.

If the body be present, just when the expiration hath ceased, either a *lāma* [who hath been as a *guru* to the deceased], or a brother in the Faith whom the deceased trusted, or a friend for whom the deceased had great affection, putting the lips close to the ear [of the body] without actually touching it,[7] should read this Great *Thödol*.

THE PRACTICAL APPLICATION OF THIS THÖDOL BY THE OFFICIANT

Now for the explaining of the *Thödol* itself:

If thou canst gather together a grand offering, offer it in worship of the Trinity. If such cannot be done, then arrange whatever can be gathered together as objects on which thou canst concentrate thy thoughts and mentally create as illimitable an offering as possible and worship.

---

5   If for any reason the corpse is not present, the *lāma* must summon the spirit of the deceased. Only with the corpse or spirit present can the deceased receive guidance through the Otherworld.

6   This is also the case in Brāhmanism.

7   It is a Tibetan and *lāmaic* belief that touching the body interferes with the departure of the consciousness-principle. If it leaves from anywhere other than the Brāhmanic Aperture on top of the head the deceased could be reborn in a non-human state

Then the 'Path of Good Wishes Invoking the Aid of the Buddhas and Bodhisattvas' should be recited seven times or thrice.

After that, the 'Path of Good Wishes Giving Protection from Fear in the *Bardo*' and the 'Path of Good Wishes for Safe Delivery from the Dangerous Pitfalls of the *Bardo*', together with the 'Root Words of the *Bardo*', are to be read distinctly and with the proper intonation.

Then this Great *Thödol* is to be read either seven times or thrice, according to the occasion. [First cometh] the setting-face-to-face [to the symptoms of death] as they occur during the moments of death; [second] the application of the great vivid reminder, the setting-face-to-face to Reality while in the Intermediate State; and third, the methods of closing the doors of the womb while in the Intermediate State when seeking rebirth.

PART I

The *Bardo* of the Moments of Death

Instructions on the Symptoms of Death, or the First Stage of the Chikhai Bardo: *The Primary Clear Light Seen at the Moment of Death*

The first, the setting-face-to-face with the Clear Light, during the Intermediate State of the Moments of Death, is:

Here [some there may be] who have listened much [to religious instructions] yet not recognized; and [some] who, though recognizing, are, nevertheless, weak in familiarity. But all classes of individuals who have received the practical teachings [called] *Guides* will, if this be applied to them, be set-face-to-face with the fundamental Clear Light; and, without any Intermediate State, they will obtain the Unborn *Dharma-Kāya*, by the Great Perpendicular Path.[1]

---

1 Curiously, spiritual emancipation and even *Nirvāṇa* can be achieved instantaneously in Northern Buddhism via the Great Perpendicular Path, without the need to enter the *Bardo*-plane or suffer in the various worlds of *saṅgsāric* existence. However, this is only possible for those who show great competence in *yoga*, much accumulated merit or excellent *karma*.

The manner of application is:

It is best if the *guru* from whom the deceased received guiding instructions can be had; but if the *guru* cannot be obtained, then a brother of the Faith; or if the latter is also unobtainable, then a learned man of the same Faith; or, should all these be unobtainable, then a person who can read correctly and distinctly ought to read this many times over. Thereby [the deceased] will be put in mind of what he had [previously] heard of the setting-face-to-face and will at once come to recognize that Fundamental Light and undoubtedly obtain Liberation.

As regards the time for the application [of these instructions]:

When the expiration hath ceased, the vital-force will have sunk into the nerve-centre of Wisdom[2] and the Knower[3] will be experiencing the Clear Light of the natural condition.[4] Then, the vital-force, being thrown backwards and flying downwards through the right and left nerves, the Intermediate State momentarily dawns.

The above [directions] should be applied before [the vital-force hath] rushed into the left nerve [after first having traversed the navel nerve-centre].

The time [ordinarily necessary for this motion of the vital-force] is as long as the inspiration is still present, or about the time required for eating a meal.[5]

Then the manner of the application [of the instructions] is:

When the breathing is about to cease, it is best if the Transference hath been applied efficiently; if [the application] hath been inefficient, then [address the deceased] thus:

2 The 'nerve-centre' referred to is psychic rather than physical. That of Wisdom is located in the heart.

3 'Knower' refers to the mind in its fully conscious state.

4 The mind in its natural, elemental state. When it is in its 'unnatural' state, it resides inside the human body and so is influenced by the five senses.

5 A unit of time, used before clocks, which lasted between twenty minutes and half an hour.

O nobly-born (so-and-so by name), the time hath now come for thee to seek the Path [in reality]. Thy breathing is about to cease. Thy *guru* hath set thee face-to-face before with the Clear Light; and now thou art about to experience it in its Reality in the *Bardo* state, wherein all things are like the void and cloudless sky, and the naked, spotless intellect is like unto a transparent vacuum without circumference or centre. At this moment, know thou thyself; and abide in that state. I, too, at this time, am setting thee face-to-face.

Having read this, repeat it many times in the ear of the person dying, even before the expiration hath ceased, so as to impress it on the mind [of the dying one].

If the expiration is about to cease, turn the dying one over on the right side, which posture is called the 'Lying Posture of a Lion'. The throbbing of the arteries [on the right and left side of the throat] is to be pressed.

If the person dying be disposed to sleep, or if the sleeping state advances, that should be arrested, and the arteries pressed gently but firmly.[6] Thereby the vital-force will not be able to return from the median-nerve and will be sure to pass out through the Brāhmanic aperture. Now the real setting-face-to-face is to be applied.

At this moment, the first [glimpsing] of the *Bardo* of the Clear Light of Reality, which is the Infallible Mind of the *Dharma-Kāya*, is experienced by all sentient beings.

The interval between the cessation of the expiration and the cessation of the inspiration is the time during which the vital-force remaineth in the median-nerve.

The common people call this the state wherein the conscious-ness-principle hath fainted away. The duration of this state is

---

6 Pressure is applied to the arteries so that the person can die fully awake, and with a full awareness of their approaching death.

uncertain. [It dependeth] upon the constitution, good or bad, and [the state of] the nerves and vital-force. In those who have had even a little practical experience of the firm, tranquil state of *dhyāna*, and in those who have sound nerves, this state continueth for a long time.[7]

In the setting-face-to-face, the repetition [of the above address to the deceased] is to be persisted in until a yellowish liquid beginneth to appear from the various apertures of the bodily organs [of the deceased].

In those who have led an evil life, and in those of unsound nerves, the above state endureth only so long as would take to snap a finger. Again, in some, it endureth as long as the time taken for the eating of a meal.

In various *Tantras* it is said that this state of swoon endureth for about three and one-half days. Most other [religious treatises] say for four days; and that this setting-face-to-face with the Clear Light ought to be persevered in [during the whole time].

The manner of applying [these directions] is:

If [when dying] one be by one's own self capable [of diagnosing the symptoms of death], use [of the knowledge] should have been made ere this. If [the dying person be] unable to do so, then either the *guru*, or a *shishya*, or a brother in the Faith with whom the one [dying] was very intimate, should be kept at hand, who will vividly impress upon the one [dying] the symptoms [of death] as they appear in due order [repeatedly saying, at first] thus:

Now the symptoms of earth sinking into water are come.[8]

When all the symptoms [of death] are about to be completed,

---

7   This can last as much as seven days, although usually it is only four or five. While the consciousness-principle tends to leave the body at the moment of death, it nonetheless retains a delicate magnetic-like connection with the physical body until this state is over.

8   One of the three main symptoms of death. The other two are 'water sinking into fire' and 'fire sinking into air'.

then enjoin upon [the one dying] this resolution, speaking in a low tone of voice in the ear:

O nobly-born (or, if it be a priest, O Venerable Sir), let not thy mind be distracted.

If it be a brother [in the Faith], or some other person, then call him by name, and [say] thus:

O nobly-born, that which is called death being come to thee now, resolve thus: 'O this now is the hour of death. By taking advantage of this death, I will so act, for the good of all sentient beings, peopling the illimitable expanse of the heavens, as to obtain the Perfect Buddhahood, by resolving on love and compassion towards [them, and by directing my entire effort to] the Sole Perfection.'

Shaping the thoughts thus, especially at this time when the *Dharma-Kāya* of Clear Light [in the state] after death can be realized for the benefit of all sentient beings, know that thou art in that state; [and resolve] that thou wilt obtain the best boon of the State of the Great Symbol,[9] in which thou art, [as follows]:

'Even if I cannot realize it, yet will I know this *Bardo*, and, mastering the Great Body of Union in *Bardo*, will appear in whatever [shape] will benefit [all beings] whomsoever: I will serve all sentient beings, infinite in number as are the limits of the sky.'

Keeping thyself unseparated from this resolution, thou shouldst try to remember whatever devotional practices thou wert accustomed to perform during thy lifetime.

In saying this, the reader shall put his lips close to the ear, and shall repeat it distinctly, clearly impressing it upon the dying person so as to prevent his mind from wandering even for a moment.

After the expiration hath completely ceased, press the nerve of

9 It is possible for the Ultimate Truth to be realized at this stage, but only if the deceased made good progress along the Path before death. Otherwise he must wander on and on down *Bardo* until rebirth.

sleep firmly; and, a *lāma*, or a person higher or more learned than thyself, impress in these words, thus:

Reverend Sir, now that thou art experiencing the Fundamental Clear Light, try to abide in that state which now thou art experiencing.

And also in the case of any other person the reader shall set him face-to-face thus:

O nobly-born (so-and-so), listen. Now thou art experiencing the Radiance of the Clear Light of Pure Reality. Recognize it. O nobly-born, thy present intellect, in real nature void, not formed into anything as regards characteristics or colour, naturally void, is the very Reality, the All-Good.

Thine own intellect, which is now voidness, yet not to be regarded as of the voidness of nothingness, but as being the intellect itself, unobstructed, shining, thrilling, and blissful, is the very consciousness, the All-good Buddha.

Thine own consciousness, not formed into anything, in reality void, and the intellect, shining and blissful – these two – are inseparable. The union of them is the *Dharma-Kāya* state of Perfect Enlightenment.[10]

Thine own consciousness, shining, void, and inseparable from the Great Body of Radiance, hath no birth, nor death, and is the Immutable Light – Buddha Amitābha.[11]

Knowing this is sufficient. Recognizing the voidness of thine own intellect to be Buddhahood, and looking upon it as being thine own consciousness, is to keep thyself in the [state of the] divine mind of the Buddha.

Repeat this distinctly and clearly three or [even] seven times. That will recall to the mind [of the dying one] the former [i.e. when living] setting-face-to-face by the *guru*.

---

10 The purest and highest state of being, devoid of limitations.

11 The state of the Boundless Light.

Secondly, it will cause the naked consciousness to be recognized as the Clear Light; and, thirdly, recognizing one's own self [thus], one becometh permanently united with the *Dharma-Kāya* and Liberation will be certain.

INSTRUCTIONS CONCERNING THE SECOND STAGE OF THE CHIKHAI BARDO: THE SECONDARY CLEAR LIGHT SEEN IMMEDIATELY AFTER DEATH

Thus the primary Clear Light is recognized and Liberation attained. But if it be feared that the primary Clear Light hath not been recognized, then [it can certainly be assumed] there is dawning [upon the deceased] that called the secondary Clear Light, which dawneth in somewhat more than a meal-time period after that the expiration hath ceased.

According to one's good or bad *karma*, the vital-force floweth down into either the right or left nerve and goeth out through any of the apertures [of the body]. Then cometh a lucid condition of the mind.

To say that the state [of the primary Clear Light] endureth for a meal-time period [would depend upon] the good or bad condition of the nerves and also whether there hath been previous practice or not [in the setting-face-to-face].

When the consciousness-principle getteth outside [the body, it sayeth to itself], 'Am I dead, or am I not dead?' It cannot determine. It seeth its relatives and connections as it had been used to seeing them before. It even heareth the wailings. The terrifying *karmic* illusions have not yet dawned. Nor have the frightful apparitions or experiences caused by the Lords of Death yet come.

During this interval, the directions are to be applied [by the *lāma* or reader]:

There are those [devotees] of the perfected stage and of the visualizing stage. If it be one who was in the perfected stage, then call him thrice by name and repeat over and over again the above instructions of setting-face-to-face with the Clear Light. If it be one who was in the visualizing stage, then read out to him the introductory descriptions and the text of the Meditation on his tutelary deity, and then say,

O thou of noble-birth, meditate upon thine own tutelary deity.[12] – [Here the deity's name is to be mentioned by the reader.] Do not be distracted. Earnestly concentrate thy mind upon thy tutelary deity. Meditate upon him as if he were the reflection of the moon in water, apparent yet in-existent [in itself]. Meditate upon him as if he were a being with a physical body.

So saying, [the reader will] impress it.

If [the deceased be] of the common folk, say, Meditate upon the Great Compassionate Lord.

By thus being set-face-to-face even those who would not be expected to recognize the *Bardo* [unaided] are undoubtedly certain to recognize it.

Persons who while living had been set-face-to-face [with the Reality] by a *guru*, yet who have not made themselves familiar with it, will not be able to recognize the Bardo clearly by themselves. Either a *guru* or a brother in the Faith will have to impress vividly such persons.

There may even be those who have made themselves familiar with the teachings, yet who, because of the violence of the disease causing death, may be mentally unable to withstand illusions. For such, also, this instruction is absolutely necessary.

Again [there are those] who, although previously familiar with the teachings, have become liable to pass into the miserable states of existence, owing to breach of vows or failure to perform essential obligations honestly. To them, this [instruction] is indispensable.

---

12 Usually one of the Buddhas or Boddhisattvas, of whom Chenrazee is the most popular.

If the first stage of the *Bardo* hath been taken by the forelock, that is best. But if not, by application of this distinct recalling [to the deceased], while in the second stage of the *Bardo*, his intellect is awakened and attaineth liberation.

While on the second stage of the *Bardo*, one's body is of the nature of that called the shining illusory-body.

Not knowing whether [he be] dead or not, [a state of] lucidity cometh [to the deceased]. If the instructions be successfully applied to the deceased while he is in that state, then, by the meeting of the Mother-Reality and the Offspring-Reality,[13] *karma* controlleth not. Like the sun's rays, for example, dispelling the darkness, the Clear Light on the Path dispelleth the power of *karma*.

That which is called the second stage of the *Bardo* dawneth upon the thought-body. The Knower hovereth within those places to which its activities had been limited. If at this time this special teaching be applied efficiently, then the purpose will be fulfilled; for the *karmic* illusions will not have come yet, and, therefore, he [the deceased] cannot be turned hither and thither [from his aim of achieving Enlightenment].

---

13 The Mother Reality is the Primal or Fundamental Truth, which can be experienced only after death. The Offspring Reality, on the other hand, can be realized in this world through practising deep meditation.

PART II

The *Bardo* of the Experiencing of Reality

Introductory Instructions Concerning the Experiencing of Reality During the Third Stage of the Bardo, *Called the* Chönyid Bardo, *when the* Karmic *Apparitions Appear*

But even though the Primary Clear Light be not recognized, the Clear Light of the second *Bardo* being recognized, Liberation will be attained. If not liberated even by that, then that called the third *Bardo* or the *Chönyid Bardo* dawneth.

In this third stage of the *Bardo*, the *karmic* illusions come to shine. It is very important that this Great Setting-face-to-face of the *Chönyid Bardo* be read: it hath much power and can do much good.

About this time [the deceased] can see that the share of food is being set aside, that the body is being stripped of its garments, that the place of the sleeping-rug is being swept; can hear all the weeping and wailing of his friends and relatives, and, although he can see them and can hear them calling upon him, they cannot hear him calling upon them, so he goeth away displeased.

At that time, sounds, lights, and rays – all three – are experienced. These awe, frighten, and terrify, and cause much fatigue. At this moment, this setting-face-to-face with the *Bardo* [during the experiencing] of Reality is to be applied. Call the deceased by name, and correctly and distinctly explain to him, as follows:

O nobly-born, listen with full attention, without being distracted. There are six states of *Bardo*, namely: the natural state of *Bardo* while in the womb; the *Bardo* of the dream-state; the *Bardo* of ecstatic equilibrium, while in deep meditation; the *Bardo* of the moment of death; the *Bardo* [during the experiencing] of Reality; the *Bardo* of the inverse process of *sangsāric* existence. These are the six.

O nobly-born, thou wilt experience three *Bardos*, the *Bardo* of the moment of death, the *Bardo* [during the experiencing] of Reality, and the *Bardo* while seeking rebirth. Of these three, up to yesterday, thou hadst experienced the *Bardo* of the moment of death. Although the Clear Light of Reality dawned upon thee, thou wert unable to hold on, and so thou hast to wander here. Now henceforth thou art going to experience the [other] two, the *Chönyid Bardo* and the *Sidpa Bardo*.

Thou wilt pay undistracted attention to that with which I am about to set thee face-to-face, and hold on:

O nobly-born, that which is called death hath now come. Thou art departing from this world, but thou art not the only one; [death] cometh to all. Do not cling, in fondness and weakness, to this life.

Even though thou clingest out of weakness, thou hast not the power to remain here. Thou wilt gain nothing more than wandering in this *Sangsāra*.[1] Be not attached [to this world]; be not weak. Remember the Precious Trinity.[2]

---

1 The endless cycle of birth, death and rebirth; literally, 'a thing whirling round'.

2 The Buddha, the Dharma and the Saṅgha.

O nobly-born, whatever fear and terror may come to thee in the *Chönyid Bardo*, forget not these words; and, bearing their meaning at heart, go forwards: in them lieth the vital secret of recognition.

'Alas! When the Uncertain Experiencing of Reality is
　　dawning upon me here,[3]
With every thought of fear or terror or awe for all [appari-
　　tional appearances] set aside,
May I recognize whatever [visions] appear, as the reflections
　　of mine own consciousness;
May I know them to be of the nature of apparitions in the
　　Bardo:
When at this all-important moment [of opportunity] of
　　achieving a great end,
May I not fear the bands of Peaceful and Wrathful [Deities],
　　mine own thought-forms.'

Repeat thou these [verses] clearly, and remembering their significance as thou repeatest them, go forwards, [O nobly-born]. Thereby,
whatever visions of awe or terror appear, recognition is certain;
and forget not this vital secret art lying therein.

O nobly-born, when thy body and mind were separating, thou
must have experienced a glimpse of the Pure Truth, subtle, sparkling,
bright, dazzling, glorious, and radiantly awesome, in appearance like
a mirage moving across a landscape in spring-time in one continuous
stream of vibrations. Be not daunted thereby, nor terrified, nor awed.
That is the radiance of thine own true nature. Recognize it.

From the midst of that radiance, the natural sound of Reality,
reverberating like a thousand thunders simultaneously sounding,

---

3　'Uncertain' because Reality is being viewed through the illusory *Bardo* counterpart of the
　　body's earthly faculties, not the pure *Dharma-Kāya* state.

will come. That is the natural sound of thine own real self. Be not daunted thereby, nor terrified, nor awed.

The body which thou hast now is called the thought-body of propensities. Since thou hast not a material body of flesh and blood, whatever may come – sounds, lights, or rays – are, all three, unable to harm thee: thou art incapable of dying. It is quite sufficient for thee to know that these apparitions are thine own thought-forms. Recognize this to be the *Bardo*.

O nobly-born, if thou dost not now recognize thine own thought-forms, whatever of meditation or of devotion thou mayst have performed while in the human world – if thou hast not met with this present teaching – the lights will daunt thee, the sounds will awe thee, and the rays will terrify thee. Shouldst thou not know this all-important key to the teachings – not being able to recognize the sounds, lights, and rays – thou wilt have to wander in the *Sangsāra*.

THE DAWNING OF THE PEACEFUL DEITIES, FROM THE FIRST TO THE SEVENTH DAY

Assuming that the deceased is *karmically* bound – as the average departed one is – to pass through the forty-nine days of the *Bardo* existence, despite the very frequent settings-face-to-face, the daily trials and dangers which he must meet and attempt to triumph over, during the first seven days, wherein dawn the Peaceful Deities, are next explained to him in detail; the first day, judging from the text, being reckoned from the time in which normally he would be expected to wake up to the fact that he is dead and on the way back to rebirth, or about three-and-one-half to four days after death.

THE FIRST DAY

O nobly-born, thou hast been in a swoon during the last three and one-half days. As soon as thou art recovered from this swoon, thou wilt have the thought, 'What hath happened!'

Act so that thou wilt recognize the *Bardo*. At that time, all the *Sangsāra* will be in revolution; and the phenomenal appearances that thou wilt see then will be the radiances and deities. The whole heavens will appear deep blue.

Then, from the Central Realm, called the Spreading Forth of the Seed, the Bhagavān Vairochana,[4] white in colour, and seated upon a lion-throne, bearing an eight-spoked wheel in his hand, and embraced by the Mother of the Space of Heaven, will manifest himself to thee.

It is the aggregate of matter resolved into its primordial state which is the blue light.

The Wisdom of the *Dharma-Dhātu*, blue in colour, shining, transparent, glorious, dazzling, from the heart of Vairochana as the Father-Mother,[5] will shoot forth and strike against thee with a light so radiant that thou wilt scarcely be able to look at it.

Along with it, there will also shine a dull white light from the *devas*, which will strike against thee in thy front.

Thereupon, because of the power of bad karma, the glorious blue light of the Wisdom of the *Dharma-Dhātu* will produce in thee fear and terror, and thou wilt [wish to] flee from it. Thou wilt beget a fondness for the dull white light of the *devas*.

At this stage, thou must not be awed by the divine blue light which will appear shining, dazzling, and glorious; and be not startled by it. That is the light of the *Tathāgata*[6] called the Light of the Wisdom of the *Dharma-Dhātu*. Put thy faith in it, believe in it firmly, and pray unto it, thinking in thy mind that it is the light proceeding from the heart of the Bhagavān Vairochana coming to receive thee while in the dangerous ambuscade of the *Bardo*. That light is the light of the grace of Vairochana.

4   'Bhagavān' means 'One Possessed of Dominion' and 'Vairochana' (lit. 'in shapes making visible') makes him the 'Manifester of Phenomena'.

5   The chief deity personifies both male and female principles of nature, hence 'Father-Mother'.

6   One who has reached the Goal or *Nirvāṇa* – a Buddha.

Be not fond of the dull white light of the *devas*. Be not attached [to it]; be not weak.

If thou be attached to it, thou wilt wander into the abodes of the *devas* and be drawn into the whirl of the Six *Lokas*. That is an interruption to obstruct thee on the Path of Liberation. Look not at it. Look at the bright blue light in deep faith. Put thy whole thought earnestly upon Vairochana and repeat after me this prayer:

'Alas! When wandering in the *Sangsāra*, because of intense
   stupidity,
On the radiant light-path of the *Dharma-Dhātu* Wisdom
May [I] be led by the Bhagavān Vairochana,
May the Divine Mother of Infinite Space be [my] rearguard;
May [I] be led safely across the fearful ambush of the *Bardo*;
May [I] be placed in the state of the All-Perfect Buddhahood.'

Praying thus, in intense humble faith, [thou] wilt merge, in halo of rainbow light, into the heart of Vairochana, and obtain Buddhahood in the *Sambhoga-Kāya*, in the Central Realm of the Densely-Packed.[7]

THE SECOND DAY

But if, notwithstanding this setting-face-to-face, through power of anger or obscuring *karma* one should be startled at the glorious light and flee, or be overcome by illusions, despite the prayer, on the Second Day, Vajra-Sattva and his attendant deities, as well as one's evil deeds [meriting] Hell, will come to receive one.

Thereupon the setting-face-to-face is, calling the deceased by name, thus:

---

7   So named because the seeds of all universal forces and things are tightly packed together
    in that place.

O nobly-born, listen undistractedly. On the Second Day the pure form of water will shine as a white light. At that time, from the deep blue Eastern Realm of Pre-eminent Happiness, the Bhagavān Akṣhobhya [as] Vajra-Sattva, blue in colour, holding in his hand a five-pronged *dorje*,[8] seated upon an elephant-throne, and embraced by the Mother Māmakī, will appear to thee, attended by the Bodhisattvas Kṣhitigarbha[9] and Maitreya,[10] with the female Bodhisattvas, Lasema and Pushpema. These six *Bodhic* deities will appear to thee.

The aggregate of thy principle of consciousness, being in its pure form – which is the Mirror-like Wisdom – will shine as a bright, radiant white light, from the heart of Vajra-Sattva, the Father-Mother, with such dazzling brilliancy and transparency that thou wilt scarcely be able to look at it, [and] will strike against thee. And a dull, smoke-coloured light from Hell will shine alongside the light of the Mirror-like Wisdom and will [also] strike against thee.

Thereupon, through the power of anger, thou wilt beget fear and be startled at the dazzling white light and wilt [wish to] flee from it; thou wilt beget a feeling of fondness for the dull smoke-coloured light from Hell. Act then so that thou wilt not fear that bright, dazzling, transparent white light. Know it to be Wisdom. Put thy humble and earnest faith in it. That is the light of the grace of the Bhagavān Vajra-Sattva. Think, with faith, 'I will take refuge in it'; and pray.

That is the Bhagavān Vajra-Sattva coming to receive thee and to save thee from the fear and terror of the *Bardo*.

Believe in it; for it is the hook of the rays of grace of Vajra-Sattva.[11]

Be not fond of the dull, smoke-coloured light from Hell. That is

---

8 The *lāmaic* sceptre, the thunderbolt of Indra.

9 'Womb (or Matrix) of the earth'.

10 Literally meaning 'love', this refers to the coming Buddha who will reform mankind through divine love.

11 A hook of salvation that draws the deceased away from the dangers of the *Bardo*.

the path which openeth out to receive thee because of the power of accumulated evil *karma* from violent anger. If thou be attracted by it, thou wilt fall into the Hell-Worlds; and, falling therein, thou wilt have to endure unbearable misery, whence there is no certain time of getting out. That being an interruption to obstruct thee on the Path of Liberation, look not at it; and avoid anger. Be not attracted by it; be not weak. Believe in the dazzling bright white light; [and] putting thy whole heart earnestly upon the Bhagavān Vajra-Sattva, pray thus:

> 'Alas! When wandering in the *Sangsāra* because of the
>   power of violent anger,
> On the radiant light-path of the Mirror-like Wisdom,
> May [I] be led by the Bhagavān Vajra-Sattva,
> May the Divine Mother Māmakī be [my] rear-guard;
> May [I] be led safely across the fearful ambush of the *Bardo*;
> And may [I] be placed in the state of the All-perfect
>   Buddhahood.'

Praying thus, in intense humble faith, thou wilt merge, in rainbow light, into the heart of the Bhagavān Vajra-Sattva and obtain Buddhahood in the *Sambhoga-Kāya*, in the Eastern Realm called Pre-eminently Happy.

THE THIRD DAY

Yet, even when set-face-to-face in this way, some persons, because of obscurations from bad *karma*, and from pride, although the hook of the rays of grace [striketh against them], flee from it. [If one be one of them], then, on the Third Day, the Bhagavān Ratna-Sambhava[12] and his accompanying deities, along with the

---

12 The Beautifier, from whom comes all that is precious; a personified characteristic of the Buddha.

light-path from the human world, will come to receive one simultaneously.

Again, calling the deceased by name, the setting-face-to-face is thus:

O nobly-born, listen undistractedly. On the Third Day the primal form of the element earth will shine forth as a yellow light. At that time, from the Southern Realm Endowed with Glory, the Bhagavān Ratna-Sambhava, yellow in colour, bearing a jewel in his hand, seated upon a horse-throne and embraced by the Divine Mother Sangyay-Chanma,[13] will shine upon thee.

The two Bodhisattvas, Ākāsha-Garbha[14] and Samanta-Bhadra,[15] attended by the two female Bodhisattvas, Mahlaima and Dhupema – in all, six *Bodhic* forms – will come to shine from amidst a rainbow halo of light. The aggregate of touch in its primal form, as the yellow light of the Wisdom of Equality, dazzlingly yellow, glorified with orbs having satellite orbs of radiance, so clear and bright that the eye can scarcely look upon it, will strike against thee. Side by side with it, the dull bluish-yellow light from the human [world] will also strike against thy heart, along with the Wisdom light.

Thereupon, through the power of egotism, thou wilt beget a fear for the dazzling yellow light and wilt [wish to] flee from it. Thou wilt be fondly attracted towards the dull bluish-yellow light from the human [world].

At that time do not fear that bright, dazzling-yellow, transparent light, but know it to be Wisdom; in that state, keeping thy mind resigned, trust in it earnestly and humbly. If thou knowest it to be the radiance of thine own intellect – although thou exertest not thy

13 'She of the Buddha Eye(s)'.

14 'Womb (or Matrix) of the Sky'.

15 The spiritual son of the Dhyānī Buddha Vairochana.

humility and faith and prayer to it – the Divine Body and Light will merge into thee inseparably, and thou wilt obtain Buddhahood.

If thou dost not recognize the radiance of thine own intellect, think, with faith, 'It is the radiance of the grace of the Bhagavān Ratna-Sambhava; I will take refuge in it'; and pray. It is the hook of the grace-rays of the Bhagavān Ratna-Sambhava; believe in it.

Be not fond of that dull bluish-yellow light from the human [world]. That is the path of thine accumulated propensities of violent egotism come to receive thee. If thou art attracted by it, thou wilt be born in the human world and have to suffer birth, age, sickness, and death; and thou wilt have no chance of getting out of the quagmire of worldly existence. That is an interruption to obstruct thy path of liberation. Therefore, look not upon it, and abandon egotism, abandon propensities; be not attracted towards it; be not weak. Act so as to trust in that bright dazzling light. Put thine earnest thought, one-pointedly, upon the Bhagavān Ratna-Sambhava; and pray thus:

'Alas! When wandering in the *Sangsāra* because of the
    power of violent egotism,
On the radiant light-path of the Wisdom of Equality,
May [I] be led by the Bhagavān Ratna-Sambhava;
May the Divine Mother, She-of-the-Buddha-Eye, be [my]
    rear-guard;
May [I] be led safely across the fearful ambush of the *Bardo*;
And may [I] be placed in the state of the All-Perfect
    Buddhahood.'

By praying thus, with deep humility and faith, thou wilt merge into the heart of the Bhagavān Ratna-Sambhava, the Divine Father-Mother, in halo of rainbow light, and attain Buddhahood in the *Sambhoga-Kāya*, in the Southern Realm Endowed with Glory.

THE FOURTH DAY

By thus being set-face-to-face, however weak the mental faculties may be, there is no doubt of one's gaining Liberation. Yet, though so often set-face-to-face, there are classes of men who, having created much bad *karma*, or having failed in observance of vows, or, their lot [for higher development] being altogether lacking, prove unable to recognize: their obscurations and evil *karma* from covetousness and miserliness produce awe of the sounds and radiances, and they flee. [If one be of these classes], then, on the Fourth Day, the Bhagavān Amitābha[16] and his attendant deities, together with the light-path from the *Preta-loka*, proceeding from miserliness and attachment, will come to receive one simultaneously.

Again, the setting-face-to-face is, calling the deceased by name, thus:

O nobly-born, listen undistractedly. On the Fourth Day the red light, which is the primal form of the element fire, will shine. At that time, from the Red Western Realm of Happiness, the Bhagavān Buddha Amitābha, red in colour, bearing a lotus in his hand, seated upon a peacock-throne and embraced by the Divine Mother Gōkarmo,[17] will shine upon thee, [together with] the Bodhisattvas Chenrazee[18] and Jampal,[19] attended by the female Bodhisattvas Ghirdhima and Āloke. The six bodies of Enlightenment will shine upon thee from amidst a halo of rainbow light.

The primal form of the aggregate of feelings as the red light of the All-Discriminating Wisdom, glitteringly red, glorified with orbs and satellite orbs, bright, transparent, glorious and dazzling,

16 An embodiment of one of the Buddha-attributes or Wisdoms, Amitābha personifies eternal life.

17 'She-in-White-Raiment'.

18 The 'Down-Looking One', the symbol of mercy or compassion. The Dalai Lāmas are seen as his incarnations.

19 'The God of Mystic Wisdom', the Buddhist Apollo.

proceeding from the heart of the Divine Father-Mother Amitābha, will strike against thy heart [so radiantly] that thou wilt scarcely be able to look upon it. Fear it not.

Along with it, a dull red light from the *Preta-loka*, coming side by side with the Light of Wisdom, will also shine upon thee. Act so that thou shalt not be fond of it. Abandon attachment [and] weakness [for it].

At that time, through the influence of intense attachment, thou wilt become terrified by the dazzling red light, and wilt [wish to] flee from it. And thou wilt beget a fondness for that dull red light of the *Preta-loka*.

At that time, be not afraid of the glorious, dazzling, transparent, radiant red light. Recognizing it as Wisdom, keeping thine intellect in a state of resignation, thou wilt merge [into it] inseparably and attain Buddhahood.

If thou dost not recognize it, think, 'It is the rays of the grace of the Bhagavān Amitābha, and I will take refuge in it'; and, trusting humbly in it, pray unto it. That is the hook-rays of the grace of the Bhagavān Amitābha. Trust in it humbly; flee not. Even if thou fleest, it will follow thee inseparably [from thyself]. Fear it not. Be not attracted towards the dull red light of the *Preta-loka*.

That is the light-path proceeding from the accumulations of thine intense attachment [to *sangsāric* existence] which hath come to receive thee. If thou be attached thereto, thou wilt fall into the World of Unhappy Spirits and suffer unbearable misery from hunger and thirst. Thou wilt have no chance of gaining Liberation[20] [therein]. That dull red light is an interruption to obstruct thee on the Path of Liberation. Be not attached to it, and abandon habitual propensities. Be not weak. Trust in the bright dazzling red light.

20 Once the deceased becomes a *preta*, or unhappy ghost, the attainment of *Nirvāṇa* is no longer possible. He must instead wait for rebirth in the human world.

In the Bhagavān Amitābha, the Father-Mother, put thy trust one-pointedly and pray thus:

'Alas! When wandering in the *Sangsāra* because of the
power of intense attachment,
On the radiant light-path of the Discriminating Wisdom
May [I] be led by the Bhagavān Amitābha;
May the Divine Mother, She-of-White-Raiment, be [my]
rear-guard;
May [I] be safely led across the dangerous ambush of the
Bardo;
And may [I] be placed in the state of the All-Perfect
Buddhahood.'

By praying thus, humbly and earnestly, thou wilt merge into the heart of the Divine Father-Mother, the Bhagavān Amitābha, in halo of rainbow-light, and attain Buddhahood in the *Sambhoga-Kāya*, in the Western Realm named Happy.

THE FIFTH DAY

It is impossible that one should not be liberated thereby. Yet, though thus set-face-to-face, sentient beings, unable through long association with propensities to abandon propensities, and, through bad *karma* and jealousy, awe and terror being produced by the sounds and radiances – the hook-rays of grace failing to catch hold of them – wander down also to the Fifth Day. [If one be such a sentient being], thereupon the Bhagavān Amogha-Siddhi,[21] with his attendant deities and the light and rays of his grace, will come to receive one. A light proceeding from the *Asura-loka*, produced by the evil passion of jealousy, will also come to receive one.

21 'Almighty Conqueror'.

The setting-face-to-face at that time is, calling the deceased by name, thus:

O nobly-born, listen undistractedly. On the Fifth Day, the green light of the primal form of the element air will shine upon thee. At that time, from the Green Northern Realm of Successful Performance of Best Actions, the Bhagavān Buddha Amogha-Siddhi, green in colour, bearing a crossed-*dorje*[22] in hand, seated upon a sky-traversing Harpy-throne,[23] embraced by the Divine Mother, the Faithful Dölma,[24] will shine upon thee, with his attendants – the two Bodhisattvas Chag-na-Dorje[25] and Ḍibpanamsel,[26] attended by two female Bodhisattvas, Gandhema and Nidhema. These six *Bodhic* forms, from amidst a halo of rainbow light, will come to shine.

The primal form of the aggregate of volition, shining as the green light of the All-Performing Wisdom, dazzlingly green, transparent and radiant, glorious and terrifying, beautified with orbs surrounded by satellite orbs of radiance, issuing from the heart of the Divine Father-Mother Amogha-Siddhi, green in colour, will strike against thy heart [so wondrously bright] that thou wilt scarcely be able to look at it. Fear it not. That is the natural power of the wisdom of thine own intellect. Abide in the state of great resignation of impartiality.

Along with it [i.e. the green light of the All-Performing Wisdom], a light of dull green colour from the *Asura-loka*, produced from the cause of the feeling of jealousy, coming side by side with the Wisdom Rays, will shine upon thee. Meditate upon it with impartiality – with neither repulsion nor attraction. Be not fond of it: if thou art of low mental capacity, be not fond of it.

---

22 A *dorje* with four heads

23 There is a Tibetan belief in harpies that are human from the waist upwards and bird-like from the waist downwards.

24 The divine consort of Avalokiteshvara.

25 'Bearing the *dorje* in hand'.

26 'Clearer of Obscurations'.

Thereupon, through the influence of intense jealousy,[27] thou wilt be terrified at the dazzling radiance of the green light and wilt [wish to] flee from it; and thou wilt beget a fondness for that dull green light of the *Asura-loka*. At that time fear not the glorious and transparent, radiant and dazzling green light, but know it to be Wisdom; and in that state allow thine intellect to rest in resignation. Or else [think], 'It is the hook-rays of the light of grace of the Bhagavān Amogha-Siddhi, which is the All-Performing Wisdom.' Believe [thus] on it. Flee not from it.

Even though thou shouldst flee from it, it will follow thee inseparably [from thyself]. Fear it not. Be not fond of that dull green light of the *Asura-loka*. That is the *karmic* path of acquired intense jealousy, which hath come to receive thee. If thou art attracted by it, thou wilt fall into the *Asura-loka* and have to engage in unbearable miseries of quarrelling and warfare. [That is an] interruption to obstruct thy path of liberation. Be not attracted by it. Abandon thy propensities. Be not weak. Trust in the dazzling green radiance, and putting thy whole thought one-pointedly upon the Divine Father-Mother, the Bhagavān Amogha-Siddhi, pray thus:

'Alas! When wandering in the *Sangsāra* because of the
    power of intense jealousy,
On the radiant light-path of the All-Performing Wisdom
May [I] be led by the Bhagavān Amogha-Siddhi;
May the Divine Mother, the Faithful Tārā, be [my] rear-guard;
May [I] be led safely across the dangerous ambush of the
    Bardo;
And may [I] be placed in the state of the All-Perfect
    Buddhahood.'

27 The *karmic* tendencies to jealousy.

By praying thus with intense faith and humility, thou wilt merge into the heart of the Divine Father-Mother, the Bhagavān Amogha-Siddhi, in halo of rainbow light, and attain Buddhahood in the *Sambhoga-Kāya*, in the Northern Realm of Heaped-up Good Deeds.

THE SIXTH DAY

Being thus set-face-to-face at various stages, however weak one's *karmic* connections may be, one should have recognized in one or the other of them; and where one has recognized in any of them it is impossible not to be liberated. Yet, although set-face-to-face so very often in that manner, one long habituated to strong propensities and lacking in familiarity with, and pure affection for, Wisdom, may be led backwards by the power of one's own evil inclinations despite these many introductions. The hook-rays of the light of grace may not be able to catch hold of one: one may still wander downwards because of one's begetting the feeling of awe and terror of the lights and rays.

Thereupon all the Divine Fathers-Mothers of the Five Orders [of Dhyāni Buddhas] with their attendants will come to shine upon one simultaneously. At the same time, the lights proceeding from the Six *Lokas* will likewise come to shine upon one simultaneously.

The setting-face-to-face for that is, calling the deceased by name, thus:

O nobly-born, until yesterday each of the Five Orders of Deities had shone upon thee, one by one; and thou hadst been set-face-to-face, but, owing to the influence of thine evil propensities, thou wert awed and terrified by them and hast remained here till now.

If thou hadst recognized the radiances of the Five Orders of Wisdom to be the emanations from thine own thought-forms, ere this thou wouldst have obtained Buddhahood in the *Sambhoga-Kāya*, through having been absorbed into the halo of rainbow light in one or another of the Five Orders of Buddhas. But now look on undistractedly. Now the lights of all Five Orders, called the Lights of the Union of Four Wisdoms, will come to receive thee. Act so as to know them.

O nobly-born, on this the Sixth Day, the four colours of the primal states of the four elements [water, earth, fire, air] will shine upon thee simultaneously. At that time, from the Central Realm of the Spreading Forth of Seed, the Buddha Vairochana, the Divine Father-Mother, with the attendant [deities], will come to shine upon thee. From the Eastern Realm of Pre-eminent Happiness, the Buddha Vajra-Sattva, the Divine Father-Mother, with the attendant [deities] will come to shine upon thee. From the Southern Realm endowed with Glory, the Buddha Ratna-Sambhava, the Divine Father-Mother, with the attendant [deities] will come to shine upon thee. From the Happy Western Realm of Heaped-up Lotuses, the Buddha Amitābha, the Divine Father-Mother, along with the attendant [deities] will come to shine upon thee. From the Northern Realm of Perfected Good Deeds, the Buddha Amogha-Siddhi, the Divine Father-Mother, along with the attendants will come, amidst a halo of rainbow light, to shine upon thee at this very moment.

O nobly-born, on the outer circle of these five pair of Dhyānī Buddhas, the [four] Door-Keepers, the Wrathful [Ones]: the Victorious One, the Destroyer of the Lord of Death, the Horse-necked King, the Urn of Nectar; with the four female Door-keepers: the Goad-Bearer, the Noose-Bearer, the Chain-Bearer, and the Bell-Bearer; along with the Buddha of the *Devas*, named the One of Supreme Power, the Buddha of the *Asuras*, named [He of] Strong Texture, the Buddha of Mankind, named the Lion of the Shākyas, the Buddha of the brute kingdom, named the Unshakable Lion, the Buddha of the *Pretas*, named the One of Flaming Mouth, and the Buddha of the Lower World, named the King of Truth: – [these], the Eight Father-Mother Door-keepers and the Six Teachers, the Victorious Ones – will come to shine, too.

The All-Good Father, and the All-Good Mother, the Great Ancestors of all the Buddhas: Samanta-Bhadra [and Samanta-Bhadrā], the Divine Father and the Divine Mother – these two, also will come to shine.

These forty-two perfectly endowed deities, issuing from within thy heart, being the product of thine own pure love, will come to shine. Know them.

O nobly-born, these realms are not come from somewhere outside [thyself]. They come from within the four divisions of thy heart, which, including its centre, make the five directions. They issue from within there, and shine upon thee. The deities, too, are not come from somewhere else: they exist from eternity within the faculties of thine own intellect.[28] Know them to be of that nature.

O nobly-born, the size of all these deities is not large, not small, [but] proportionate. [They have] their ornaments, their colours, their sitting postures, their thrones, and the emblems that each holds.

These deities are formed into groups of five pairs, each group of five being surrounded by a fivefold circle of radiances, the male Bodhisattvas partaking of the nature of the Divine Fathers, and the female Bodhisattvas partaking of the nature of the Divine Mothers. All these divine conclaves will come to shine upon thee in one complete conclave. They are thine own tutelary deities.[29] Know them to be such.

O nobly-born, from the hearts of the Divine Fathers and Mothers of the Five Orders, the rays of light of the Four Wisdoms united, extremely clear and fine, like the rays of the sun spun into threads, will come and shine upon thee and strike against thy heart.

On that path of radiance there will come to shine glorious orbs of light, blue in colour, emitting rays, the *Dharma-Dhātu* Wisdom

28 In Northern Buddhism, man is the microcosm of the macrocosm.

29 They are the visualizations of the individual who believes in them.

[itself], each appearing like an inverted turquoise cup, surrounded by similar orbs, smaller in size, glorious and dazzling, radiant and transparent, each made more glorious with five yet smaller [satellite] orbs dotted round about with five starry spots of light of the same nature, leaving neither the centre nor the borders [of the blue light-path] unglorified by the orbs and the smaller [satellite] orbs.

From the heart of Vajra-Sattva, the white light-path of the Mirror-like Wisdom, white and transparent, glorious and dazzling, glorious and terrifying, made more glorious with orbs surrounded by smaller orbs of transparent and radiant light upon it, each like an inverted mirror, will come to shine. From the heart of Ratna-Sambhava, the yellow light-path of the Wisdom of Equality, [glorified] with yellow orbs [of radiance], each like an inverted gold cup, surrounded by smaller orbs, and these with yet smaller orbs, will come to shine.

From the heart of Amitābha, the transparent, bright red light-path of the Discriminating Wisdom, upon which are orbs, like inverted coral cups, emitting rays of Wisdom, extremely bright and dazzling, each glorified with five [satellite] orbs of the same nature – leaving neither the centre nor the borders [of the red light-path] unglorified with orbs and smaller satellite orbs – will come to shine.

These will come to shine against thy heart simultaneously.[30]

O nobly-born, all those are the radiances of thine own intellectual faculties come to shine. They have not come from any other place. Be not attracted towards them; be not weak; be not terrified; but abide in the mood of non-thought-formation.[31]

---

30 Each of these mystical lights represents the specific *Bodhic*, or Wisdom, quality of the Buddha from which it emanates.

31 Non-thought-formation is achieved in *samādhi-yoga*. Thought-formation curtails the natural flow of the mind, just as a leaf carried along with the current of a river is stopped by a protruding rock.

In that state all the forms and radiances will merge into thyself, and Buddhahood will be obtained.

The green light-path of the Wisdom of Perfected Actions will not shine upon thee, because the Wisdom-faculty of thine intellect hath not been perfectly developed.

O nobly-born, those are called the Lights of the Four Wisdoms United, [whence proceeds that] which is called the Inner Path through Vajra-Sattva.[32]

At that time, thou must remember the teachings of the setting-face-to-face which thou hast had from thy *guru*. If thou hast remembered the purport of the settings-face-to-face, thou wilt have recognized all these lights which have shone upon thee, as being the reflection of thine own inner light, and, having recognized them as intimate friends, thou wilt have believed in them and have understood [them at] the meeting, as a son understandeth his mother.

And believing in the unchanging nature of the pure and holy Truth, thou wilt have had produced in thee the tranquil-flowing *Samādhi*; and, having merged into the body of the perfectly evolved intellect, thou wilt have obtained Buddhahood in the *Sambhoga-Kāya*, whence there is no return.

O nobly-born, along with the radiances of Wisdom, the impure illusory lights of the Six *Lokas* will also come to shine. If it be asked, 'What are they?' [they are] a dull white light from the *devas*, a dull green light from the *asuras*, a dull yellow light from human beings, a dull blue light from the brutes, a dull reddish light from the *pretas*, and a dull smoke-coloured light from Hell. These six thus will come to shine, along with the six radiances of Wisdom; whereupon, be not afraid of nor be attracted towards any, but allow thyself to rest in the non-thought condition.

---

32 On this path in the state of Buddhahood, all the Peaceful and Wrathful Deities of the greater *mandala* merge in at-one-ment.

If thou art frightened by the pure radiances of Wisdom and attracted by the impure lights of the Six *Lokas*, then thou wilt assume a body in any of the Six *Lokas* and suffer *sangsāric* miseries; and thou wilt never be emancipated from the Ocean of *Sangsāra*, wherein thou wilt be whirled round and round and made to taste of the sufferings thereof.

O nobly-born, if thou art one who hath not obtained the select words of the *guru*, thou wilt have fear of the pure radiances of Wisdom and of the deities thereof. Being thus frightened, thou wilt be attracted towards the impure *sangsāric* objects. Act not so. Humbly trust in the dazzling pure radiances of Wisdom. Frame thy mind to faith, and think, 'The compassionate radiances of Wisdom of the Five Orders of Buddhas have come to take hold of me out of compassion; I take refuge in them.'

Not yielding to attraction towards the illusory lights of the Six *Lokas*, but devoting thy whole mind one-pointedly towards the Divine Fathers and Mothers, the Buddhas of the Five Orders, pray thus:

'Alas! When wandering in the *Sangsāra* through the power
    of the five virulent poisons,[33]
On the bright radiance-path of the Four Wisdoms united,
May [I] be led by the Five Victorious Conquerors,
May the Five Orders of Divine Mothers be [my] rear-guard;
May [I] be rescued from the impure light-paths of the Six
    Lokas;
And, being saved from the ambuscades of the dread *Bardo*,
May [I] be placed within the five pure Divine Realms.'

By thus praying, one recognizeth one's own inner light; and,

33 They are lust, hatred, stupidity, pride or vanity and jealousy.

merging one's self therein, in at-one-ment, Buddhahood is attained: through humble faith, the ordinary devotee cometh to know himself, and obtaineth Liberation; even the most lowly, by the power of the pure prayer, can close the doors of the Six *Lokas*, and, in understanding the real meaning of the Four Wisdoms united, obtain Buddhahood by the hollow pathway through Vajra-Sattva.[34]

Thus by being set-face-to-face in that detailed manner, those who are destined to be liberated will come to recognize [the Truth];[35] thereby many will attain Liberation.

The worst of the worst, [those] of heavy evil *karma*, having not the least predilection for any religion – and some who have failed in their vows – through the power of *karmic* illusions, not recognizing, although set-face-to-face [with Truth], will stray downwards.

THE SEVENTH DAY

On the Seventh Day, the Knowledge-Holding Deities, from the holy paradise realms, come to receive one. Simultaneously, the pathway to the brute world, produced by the obscuring passion, stupidity, also cometh to receive one. The setting-face-to-face at that time is, calling the deceased by name, thus:

O nobly-born, listen undistractedly. On the Seventh Day the vari-coloured radiance of the purified propensities will come to shine. Simultaneously, the Knowledge-Holding Deities, from the holy paradise realms, will come to receive one.

From the centre of the Circle [or *Maṇḍala*], enhaloed in radiance of rainbow light, the supreme Knowledge-Holding [Deity], the Lotus Lord of Dance, the Supreme Knowledge-Holder Who Ripens *Karmic* Fruits, radiant with all the five colours, embraced by the

---

34 Vajra-Sattva represents the Void, through which the pathway to Liberation runs.

35 The Truth is that the phenomena of the *Bardo*-plane are not real. They are just the illusions stored in one's mind from *sangsāric* experiences. Recognition of this fact is followed by Liberation.

[Divine] Mother, the Red *Ḍākinī*,[36] [he] holding a crescent knife and a skull [filled] with blood,[37] dancing and making the *mudrā*[38] of fascination, [with his right hand held] aloft, will come to shine.

To the east of that Circle, the deity called the Earth-Abiding Knowledge-Holder, white of colour, with radiant smiling countenance, embraced by the White *Ḍākinī*, the [Divine] Mother, [he] holding a crescent knife and a skull [filled] with blood, dancing and making the *mudrā* of fascination, [with his right hand held] aloft, will come to shine.

To the south of that Circle, the Knowledge-Holding Deity called [He] Having Power Over Duration of Life, yellow in colour, smiling and radiant, embraced by the Yellow *Ḍākinī*, the [Divine] Mother, [he] holding a crescent knife and a skull [filled] with blood, dancing and making the *mudrā* of fascination, [with his right hand held] aloft, will come to shine.

To the west of that Circle, the deity called the Knowledge-Holding Deity of the Great Symbol, red of colour, smiling and radiant, embraced by the Red *Ḍākinī*, the [Divine] Mother, [he] holding a crescent-knife and a skull [filled] with blood, dancing and making the *mudrā* of fascination, [with his right hand held] aloft, will come to shine.

To the north of that Circle, the deity called the Self-Evolved Knowledge-Holder, green of colour, with a half-angry, half-smiling radiant countenance, embraced by the Green *Ḍākinī*, the [Divine] Mother, [he] holding a crescent-knife and a skull [filled] with blood, dancing and making the *mudrā* of fascination, [with his right hand held] aloft, will come to shine.

---

36 The *Ḍākinīs* are fairy-like goddesses with strange occult powers which can be used for good or evil.

37 Filling the skull with blood symbolizes the renunciation of both human life and the *Sangsāra*, and self-sacrifice on the cross of the world.

38 A *mudrā* is a mystic sign made using the hand and fingers or the body.

In the Outer Circle, round about these Knowledge-Holders, innumerable bands of *ḍākinīs* – *ḍākinīs* of the eight places of cremation, *ḍākinīs* of the four classes, *ḍākinīs* of the three abodes, *ḍākinīs* of the thirty holy-places and of the twenty-four places of pilgrimage – heroes, heroines, celestial warriors and faith-protecting deities, male and female, each bedecked with the six bone-ornaments, having drums and thigh-bone trumpets, skull-timbrels, banners of gigantic human[-like] hides,[39] human-hide canopies, human-hide bannerettes, fumes of human-fat incense, and innumerable [other] kinds of musical instruments, filling [with music] the whole world-systems and causing them to vibrate, to quake and tremble with sounds so mighty as to daze one's brain, and dancing various measures, will come to receive the faithful and punish the unfaithful.[40]

O nobly-born, five-coloured radiances, of the Wisdom of the Simultaneously-Born, which are the purified propensities, vibrating and dazzling like coloured threads, flashing, radiant, and transparent, glorious and awe-inspiring, will issue from the hearts of the five chief Knowledge-Holding Deities and strike against thy heart, so bright that the eye cannot bear to look upon them.

At the same time, a dull blue light from the brute world will come to shine along with the Radiances of Wisdom. Then, through the influence of the illusions of thy propensities, thou wilt feel afraid of the radiance of the five colours; and [wishing to] flee from it, thou wilt feel attracted towards the dull light from the brute-world. Thereupon, be not afraid of that brilliant radiance of five colours, nor terrified; but know the Wisdom to be thine own.

---

39 The hides of *rākṣasas*, enormous demoniacal creatures with human form and supernormal powers.

40 Tibetan *lāmas* use seven or eight kinds of instruments, which, they say, psychically produce deep respect and faith in the devotee. The sounds are the counterparts of those of the human body, which can be heard when the ears are stopped up by the fingers.

Within those radiances, the natural sound of the Truth will reverberate like a thousand thunders. The sound will come with a rolling reverberation, [amidst which] will be heard, 'Slay! Slay!' and awe-inspiring *mantras*. Fear not. Flee not. Be not terrified. Know them [i.e. these sounds] to be [of] the intellectual faculties of thine own [inner] light.

Be not attracted towards the dull blue light of the brute-world; be not weak. If thou art attracted, thou wilt fall into the brute-world, wherein stupidity predominates, and suffer the illimitable miseries of slavery and dumbness and stupidness; and it will be a very long time ere thou canst get out. Be not attracted towards it. Put thy faith in the bright, dazzling, five-coloured radiance. Direct thy mind one-pointedly towards the deities, the Knowledge-Holding Conquerors. Think, one-pointedly, thus: 'These Knowledge-Holding Deities, the Heroes, and the *Ḍākinīs* have come from the holy paradise realms to receive me; I supplicate them all: up to this day, although the Five Orders of the Buddhas of the Three Times have all exerted the rays of their grace and compassion, yet have I not been rescued by them. Alas, for a being like me! May the Knowledge-Holding Deities not let me go downwards further than this, but hold me with the hook of their compassion, and lead me to the holy paradises.'

Thinking in that manner, one-pointedly, pray thus:

'O ye Knowledge-Holding Deities, pray hearken unto me;
Lead me on the Path, out of your great love,
When [I am] wandering in the *Sangsāra*, because of intensified propensities,
On the bright light-path of the Simultaneously-born Wisdom
May the bands of Heroes, the Knowledge-Holders, lead me;
May the bands of the Mothers, the *Ḍākinīs*, be [my] rear-guard;
May they save me from the fearful ambuscades of the *Bardo*,
And place me in the pure Paradise Realms.'

Praying thus, in deep faith and humility, there is no doubt that one will be born within the pure Paradise Realms, after being merged, in rainbow-light, into the heart of the Knowledge-Holding Deities.

All the pandit classes, too, coming to recognize at this stage, obtain liberation; even those of evil propensities being sure to be liberated here.

Here endeth the part of the Great *Thödol* concerned with the setting-face-to-face of the Peaceful [Deities] of the *Chönyid Bardo* and the setting-face-to-face of the Clear Light of the *Chikhai Bardo*.

THE DAWNING OF THE WRATHFUL DEITIES, FROM THE EIGHTH TO THE FOURTEENTH DAY

INTRODUCTION

Now the manner of the dawning of the Wrathful Deities is to be shown.

In the above *Bardo* of the Peaceful [Deities] there were seven stages of ambuscade. The setting-face-to-face at each stage should have [caused the deceased] to recognize either at one or another [stage] and to have been liberated.

Multitudes will be liberated by that recognition; [and] although multitudes obtain liberation in that manner, the number of sentient beings being great, evil *karma* powerful, obscurations dense, propensities of too long standing, the Wheel of Ignorance and Illusion becometh neither exhausted nor accelerated. Although [all be] set-face-to-face in such detail, there is a vast preponderance of those who wander downwards unliberated.

Therefore, after the cessation [of the dawning] of the Peaceful and the Knowledge-Holding Deities, who come to welcome one, the fifty-eight flame-enhaloed, wrathful, blood-drinking deities come to dawn, who are only the former Peaceful Deities in changed aspect – according to the place [or psychic-centre of the *Bardo*-body of the deceased whence they proceed]; nevertheless, they will not resemble them.

This is the *Bardo* of the Wrathful Deities; and, they being influenced by fear, terror, and awe,[41] recognition becometh more difficult. The intellect, gaining not in independence, passeth from one fainting state to a round of fainting states. [Yet], if one but recognize a little, it is easier to be liberated [at this stage]. If it be asked why? [the answer is]: Because of the dawning of the radiances – [which produce] fear, terror, and awe – the intellect is undistractedly alert in one-pointedness; that is why.

If at this stage one does not meet with this kind of teaching, one's hearing [of religious lore] – although it be like an ocean [in its vastness] – is of no avail. There are even discipline-holding abbots [or *bhikkhus*] and doctors in metaphysical discourses who err at this stage, and, not recognizing, wander into the *Sangsāra*.

As for the common worldly folk, what need is there to mention them! By fleeing, through fear, terror, and awe, they fall over the precipices into the unhappy worlds and suffer. But the least of the least of the devotees of the mystic *mantrayāna* doctrines, as soon as he sees these blood-drinking deities, will recognize them to be his tutelary deities, and the meeting will be like that of human acquaintances. He will trust them; and becoming merged into them, in at-one-ment, will obtain Buddhahood.[42]

By having meditated on the description of these blood-drinking deities, while in the human world, and by having performed some

41 Fear, terror and awe will only be felt by the ordinary deceased devotee. Those adept in yoga know that the *Bardo* is an illusion, so they can expect rebirth or even *Nirvāṇa*.

42 The blood represents *sangsāric* existence. If the devotee realizes that these deities are the karmic personifications of his own disposition, the true nature of *sangsāric* existence will dawn and Buddhahood will follow.

worship or praise of them; or, at least, by having seen their painted likenesses and their images, upon witnessing the dawning of the deities at this stage, recognition of them will result, and liberation. In this lieth the art.

Again, at the death of those discipline-holding abbots and doctors in metaphysical discourses [who remain uninstructed in these *Bardo* teachings], however assiduously they may have devoted themselves to religious practices, and however clever they may have been in expounding doctrines while in the human world, there will not come any phenomenal signs such as rainbow-halo [at the funeral-pyre] nor bone-reliques [from the ashes]. This is because when they lived the mystic [or esoteric] doctrines were never held within their heart, and because they had spoken contemptuously of them, and because they were never acquainted [through initiation] with the deities of the mystic [or esoteric] doctrines; thus, when these dawn in the *Bardo*, they do not recognize them. Suddenly [seeing] what they had never seen before, they view it as inimical; and, an antagonistic feeling being engendered, they pass into the miserable states because of that. Therefore, if the observers of the disciplines, and the metaphysicians, have not in them the practices of the mystic [or esoteric] doctrines, such signs as the rainbow-halo come not, nor are bone-reliques and seed-like bones ever produced [from the bones of their funeral-pyre]: these are the reasons for it.

The least of the least of *mantrayānic* [devotees] – who may seem to be of very unrefined manners, unindustrious, untactful, and who may not live in accordance with his vows, and who in every way may be inelegant in his habits, and even unable, perhaps, to carry the practices of his teachings to a successful issue – let no one feel disrespect for nor doubt him, but pay reverence to the esoteric [or mystic] doctrines [which he holdeth]. By that, alone, one obtaineth liberation at this stage.

Even though the deeds [of one paying such reverence] may not have been very elegant while in the human world, at his death there will come at least one kind of sign, such as rainbow-radiance, bone-images, and bone-reliques. This is because the esoteric [or mystic] doctrines possess great gift-waves.

[Those of, and] above, the mystic *mantrayānic* devotees of ordinary [psychic development], who have meditated upon the visualization and perfection processes and practised the essences [or essence *mantras*], need not wander down this far on the *Chönyid Bardo*.

As soon as they cease to breathe, they will be led into the pure paradise realms by the Heroes and Heroines and the Knowledge-Holders. As a sign of this, the sky will be cloudless; they will merge into rainbow radiance; there will be sun-showers, sweet scent of incense [in the air], music in the skies, radiances; bone-reliques and images [from their funeral-pyre].

Therefore, to the abbots [or discipline-holders], to the doctors, and to those mystics who have failed in their vows, and to all the common people, this *Thödol* is indispensable. But those who have meditated upon the Great Perfection and the Great Symbol[43] will recognize the Clear Light at the moment of death; and, obtaining the *Dharma-Kāya*, all of them will be such as not to need the reading of this *Thödol*. By recognizing the Clear Light at the moment of death, they also will recognize the visions of the Peaceful and the Wrathful during the *Chönyid Bardo*, and obtain the *Sambhoga-Kāya*; or, recognizing during the *Sidpa Bardo*, obtain the *Nirmāṇa-Kāya*; and, taking birth on the higher planes, will, in the next rebirth, meet with this Doctrine, and then enjoy the continuity of *karma*.

Therefore, this *Thödol* is the doctrine by which Buddhahood may be attained without meditation; the doctrine liberating by the

43 'The Great Perfection' refers to the fundamental doctrine concerning the gaining of Buddhahood, taught by the School of *Guru* Padma Sambhava. 'The Great Symbol' refers to an ancient Indian system of yoga.

hearing [of it] alone; the doctrine which leadeth brings of great evil *karma* on the Secret Path; the doctrine which produceth differentiation instantaneously [between those who are initiated into it and those who are not]: being the profound doctrine which conferreth Perfect Enlightenment instantaneously. Those sentient beings who have been reached by it cannot go to the unhappy states.

This [doctrine] and the *Tahdol* [doctrine],[44] when joined together being like unto a *maṇḍala* of gold inset with turquoise, combine them.

Thus, the indispensable nature of the *Thödol* being shown, there now cometh the setting-face-to-face with the dawning of the Wrathful [Deities] in the *Bardo*.

THE EIGHTH DAY

Again, calling the deceased by name, [address him] thus:

O nobly-born, listen undistractedly. Not having been able to recognize when the Peaceful [Deities] shone upon thee in the *Bardo* above, thou hast come wandering thus far. Now, on the Eighth Day, the blood-drinking Wrathful Deities will come to shine. Act so as to recognize them without being distracted.

O nobly-born, the Great Glorious Buddha-Heruka, dark-brown of colour; with three heads, six hands, and four feet firmly postured; the right [face] being white, the left, red, the central, dark-brown; the body emitting flames of radiance; the nine eyes widely opened, in terrifying gaze; the eyebrows quivering like lightning; the protruding teeth glistening and set over one another; giving vent to sonorous utterances of 'a-la-la' and 'ha-ha', and piercing whistling sounds; the hair of a reddish-yellow colour, standing on end, and emitting radiance; the heads adorned with dried [human] skulls, and the [symbols of the] sun and moon; black serpents and raw

---

44 A small Tibetan work consisting entirely of *mantras*, used as an accompaniment to the *Bardo Thödol*.

[human] heads forming a garland for the body; the first of the right hands holding a wheel, the middle one, a sword, the last one, a battle-axe; the first of the left hands, a bell, the middle one, a skull-bowl, the last one, a ploughshare; his body embraced by the Mother, Buddha-Krotishaurima, her right hand clinging to his neck and her left putting to his mouth a red shell [filled with blood], [making] a palatal sound like a crackling [and] a clashing sound, and a rumbling sound as loud as thunder; [emanating from the two deities] radiant flames of wisdom, blazing from every hair-pore [of the body] and each containing a flaming *dorje*; [the two deities together thus], standing with [one] leg bent and [the other] straight and tense, on a dais supported by horned eagles,[45] will come forth from within thine own brain and shine vividly upon thee. Fear that not. Be not awed. Know it to be the embodiment of thine own intellect. As it is thine own tutelary deity, be not terrified. Be not afraid, for in reality it is the Bhagavān Vairochana, the Father-Mother. Simultaneously with the recognition, liberation will be obtained: if they be recognized, merging [thyself], in at-one-ment, into the tutelary deity, Buddhahood in the *Sambhoga-Kāya* will be won.

THE NINTH DAY

But if one flee from them, through awe and terror being begotten, then, on the Ninth Day, the blood-drinking [deities] of the Vajra Order will come to receive one. Thereupon, the setting-face-to-face is, calling the deceased by name, thus:

O nobly-born, listen undistractedly. [He] of the blood-drinking Vajra Order named the Bhagavān Vajra-Heruka, dark-blue in colour; with three faces, six hands, and four feet firmly postured; in the first right hand [holding] a *dorje*, in the middle [one], a skull-bowl, in the last [one], a battle-axe; in the first of the left, a bell, in the

---

45 The *Garudas*, which in Indian and Tibetan mythology personify energy and aspiration.

middle [one] a skull-bowl, in the last [one], a ploughshare: his body embraced by the Mother Vajra-Krotishaurima, her right [hand] clinging to his neck, her left offering to his mouth a red shell [filled with blood], will issue from the eastern quarter of thy brain and come to shine upon thee. Fear it not. Be not terrified. Be not awed. Know it to be the embodiment of thine own intellect. As it is thine own tutelary deity, be not terrified. In reality [they are] the Bhagavān Vajra-Sattva, the Father and Mother. Believe in them. Recognizing them, liberation will be obtained at once. By so proclaiming [them], knowing them to be tutelary deities, merging [in them] in at-one-ment, Buddhahood will be obtained.

THE TENTH DAY

Yet, if one do not recognize them, the obscurations of evil deeds being too great, and flee from them through terror and awe, then, on the Tenth Day, the blood-drinking [deities] of the [Precious]-Gem Order will come to receive one. Thereupon the setting-face-to-face is, calling the deceased by name, thus:

O nobly-born, listen. On the Tenth Day, the blood-drinking [deity] of the [Precious]-Gem Order named Ratna-Heruka, yellow of colour; [having] three faces, six hands, four feet firmly postured; the right [face] white, the left, red, the central darkish yellow; enhaloed in flames; in the first of the six hands holding a gem, in the middle [one], a trident-staff, in the last [one], a baton; in the first of the left [hands], a bell, in the middle [one], a skull-bowl, in the last [one], a trident-staff; his body embraced by the Mother Ratna-Krotishaurima, her right [hand] clinging to his neck, her left offering to his mouth a red shell [filled with blood], will issue from the southern quarter of thy brain and come to shine upon thee. Fear not. Be not terrified. Be not awed. Know them to be the embodiment of thine own intellect. [They] being thine own tutelary deity, be not terrified. In reality [they are] the Father-Mother Bhagavān

Ratna-Sambhava. Believe in them. Recognition [of them] and the obtaining of liberation will be simultaneous.

By so proclaiming [them], knowing them to be tutelary deities, merging in them in at-one-ment, Buddhahood will be obtained.

THE ELEVENTH DAY

Yet, though set-face-to-face thus, if, through power of evil propensities, terror and awe being produced, not recognizing them to be tutelary deities, one flee from them, then, on the Eleventh Day, the blood-drinking Lotus Order will come to receive one. Thereupon the setting-face-to-face is, calling the deceased by name, thus:

O nobly-born, on the Eleventh Day, the blood-drinking [deity] of the Lotus Order, called the Bhagavān Padma-Heruka, of reddish-black colour; [having] three faces, six hands, and four feet firmly postured; the right [face] white, the left, blue, the central, darkish red; in the first of the right of the six hands holding a lotus, in the middle [one], a trident-staff, in the last, a club; in the first of the left [hands], a bell, in the middle [one], a skull-bowl filled with blood,[46] in the last, a small drum; his body embraced by the Mother Padma-Krotishaurima, her right hand clinging to his neck, her left offering to his mouth a red shell [full of blood]; the Father and Mother in union; will issue from the western quarter of thy brain and come to shine upon thee. Fear that not. Be not terrified. Be not awed. Rejoice. Recognize [them] to be the product of thine own intellect; as [they are] thine own tutelary deity, be not afraid. In reality they are the Father-Mother Bhagavān Amitābha. Believe in them. Concomitantly with recognition, liberation will come. Through such acknowledging, recognizing them to be tutelary deities, in at-one-ment thou wilt merge [into them], and obtain Buddhahood.

---

46 In *lāmaic* rituals a fluid red pigment is used to represent blood, which symbolizes the renunciation of life or of *sangsāric* existence.

THE TWELFTH DAY

Despite such setting-face-to-face, being still led backwards by evil propensities, terror and awe arising, it may be that one recognize not and flee. Thereupon, on the Twelfth Day, the blood-drinking deities of the Karmic Order, accompanied by the Kerima, Htamenma, and Wang-chugma,[47] will come to receive one. Not recognizing, terror may be produced. Whereupon, the setting-face-to-face is, calling the deceased by name, thus:

O nobly-born, on the Twelfth Day, the blood-drinking deity of the Karmic Order, named Karma-Heruka, dark green of colour; [having] three faces, six hands, [and] four feet firmly postured; the right [face] white, the left, red, the middle, dark green; majestic [of appearance]; in the first of the right of the six hands, holding a sword, in the middle [one], a trident-staff, in the last, a club; in the first of the left [hands], a bell, in the middle [one], a skull-bowl, in the last, a ploughshare; his body embraced by the Mother Karma-Krotishaurima, her right [hand] clinging to his neck, the left offering to his mouth a red shell; the Father and Mother in union, issuing from the northern quarter of thy brain, will come to shine upon thee. Fear that not. Be not terrified. Be not awed. Recognize them to be the embodiment of thine own intellect. [They] being thine own tutelary deity, be not afraid. In reality they are the Father-Mother Bhagavān Amogha-Siddhi. Believe; and be humble; and be fond [of them]. Concomitantly with recognition, liberation will come. Through such acknowledging, recognizing them to be tutelary deities, in at-one-ment thou wilt merge [into them], and obtain Buddhahood. Through the *guru*'s select teaching, one cometh to recognize them to be the thought-forms issuing from one's own

---

47 These three orders of deities originate in India and Tibet. The Kerima has human shape and the Htamenma and Wang-chugma have human-like bodies and animal heads. Each deity symbolizes a particular *karmic* impulse and appears as a hallucination in the *Bardo* consciousness of the deceased.

intellectual faculties. For instance, a person, upon recognizing a lion-skin [to be a lion-skin], is freed [from fear]; for though it be only a stuffed lion-skin, if one do not know it to be so actually, fear ariseth, but, upon being told by some person that it is a lion-skin only, one is freed from fear. Similarly here, too, when the bands of blood-drinking deities, huge of proportions, with very thick-set limbs, dawn as big as the skies, awe and terror are naturally produced in one. [But] as soon as the setting-face-to-face is heard [one] recognizeth them to be one's own tutelary deities and one's own thought-forms. Then, when upon the Mother Clear-Light – which one had been accustomed to formerly – a secondary Clear-Light, the Offspring Clear-Light, is produced, and the Mother and Offspring Clear-Light, coming together like two intimate acquaintances, blend inseparably, and [therefrom] a self-emancipating radiance dawneth upon one, through self-enlightenment and self-knowledge one is liberated.

THE THIRTEENTH DAY

If this setting-face-to-face be not obtained, good persons on the Path, too, fall back from here and wander into the *Sangsāra*. Then the Eight Wrathful Ones, the Kerimas, and the Htamenmas, having various [animal] heads, issue from within one's own brain and come to shine upon one's self. Thereupon the setting-face-to-face is, calling the deceased by name, thus:

O nobly-born, listen undistractedly. On the Thirteenth Day, from the eastern quarter of thy brain, the Eight Kerimas will emanate and come to shine upon thee. Fear that not.

From the east of thy brain, the White Kerima,[48] holding a human corpse, as a club, in the right [hand]; in the left, holding a skull-bowl filled with blood, will come to shine upon thee. Fear not.

48 An Indian cemetery goddess.

From the south, the Yellow Tseurima,[49] holding a bow and arrow, ready to shoot; from the west, the Red Pramoha, holding a *makara*[50]-banner; from the north, the Black Petali, holding a *dorje* and a blood-filled skull-bowl; from the south-east, the Red Pukkase, holding intestines in the right [hand] and [with] the left putting them to her mouth; from the south-west, the Dark-Green Ghasmarī, the left [hand] holding a blood-filled skull-bowl, [with] the right stirring it with a *dorje*, and [she then] drinking it with majestic relish; from the north-west, the Yellowish-White Tsandhalî,[51] tearing asunder a head from a corpse, the right [hand] holding a heart, the left putting the corpse to the mouth and [she then] eating [thereof]; from the north-east, the Dark-Blue Smasha, tearing asunder a head from a corpse and eating [thereof]: these, the Eight Kerimas of the Abodes [or Eight Directions], also come to shine upon thee, surrounding the Five Blood-drinking Fathers. Yet be not afraid.

O nobly-born, from the Circle outside of them, the Eight Htamenmas of the [eight] regions [of the brain] will come to shine upon thee: from the east, the Dark-Brown Lion-Headed One, the hands crossed on the breast, and in the mouth holding a corpse, and shaking the mane; from the south, the Red Tiger-Headed One, the hands crossed downwards, grinning and showing the fangs and looking on with protruding eyes; from the west, the Black Fox-Headed One, the right [hand] holding a shaving-knife, the left holding an intestine, and [she] eating and licking the blood [therefrom]; from the north, the Dark-Blue Wolf-Headed One, the two hands tearing open a corpse and looking on with protruding eyes; from the south-east, the Yellowish-White Vulture-Headed One, bearing a gigantic [human-shaped] corpse on the shoulder and

49 An Indian cemetery goddess.

50 Water-lion' or 'leviathan', a mythological monster.

51 The spirit of a female of low caste who haunts cemeteries. Intended as a symbol to demonstrate the nature of *sangsāric* existence and the need to transcend it.

holding a skeleton in the hand; from the south-west, the Dark-Red Cemetery-Bird-Headed One, carrying a gigantic corpse on the shoulder; from the north-west, the Black Crow-Headed One, the left [hand] holding a skull-bowl, the right holding a sword, and [she] eating heart and lungs; from the north-east, the Dark-Blue Owl-Headed One, holding a *dorje* in the right [hand], and holding a sword in the left, and eating.

These Eight Htamenmas of the [eight] regions, likewise surrounding the Blood-Drinking Fathers, and issuing from within thy brain, come to shine upon thee. Fear that not. Know them to be the thought-forms of thine own intellectual faculties.

THE FOURTEENTH DAY

O nobly-born on the Fourteenth Day, the Four Female Door-Keepers, also issuing from within thine own brain, will come to shine upon thee. Again recognize. From the east [quarter] of thy brain will come to shine the White Tiger-Headed Goad-Holding Goddess, bearing a blood-filled skull-bowl in her left [hand]; from the south, the Yellow Sow-Headed Noose-Holding Goddess; from the west, the Red Lion-Headed Iron-Chain-Holding Goddess; and from the north, the Green Serpent-Headed Bell-Holding Goddess. Thus, issue the Four Female Door-Keepers also from within thine own brain and come to shine upon thee; as tutelary deities, recognize them.

O nobly-born, on the outer Circle of these thirty wrathful deities, Herukas, the twenty-eight various-headed mighty goddesses, bearing various weapons, issuing from within thine own brain, will come to shine upon thee. Fear that not.

Recognize whatever shineth to be the thought-forms of thine own intellectual faculties. At this vitally important time, recollect the select teachings of the *guru*.

O nobly-born, [there will dawn] from the east the Dark-Brown Yak-Headed Rākṣhasa-Goddess, holding a *dorje* and a skull; and the Reddish-Yellow Serpent-Headed Brāhma-Goddess, holding a lotus in her hand; and the Greenish-Black Leopard-Headed Great-Goddess, holding a trident in her hand; and the Blue Monkey-Headed Goddess of Inquisitiveness, holding a wheel; and the Red Snow-Bear-Headed Virgin-Goddess, bearing a short spear in the hand; and the White Bear-Headed Indra-Goddess, holding an intestine-noose in the hand: [these], the Six Yoginīs of the East, issuing from within the [eastern quarter of thine own] brain, will come to shine upon thee; fear that not.

O nobly-born, from the south [will dawn] the Yellow Bat-Headed Delight-Goddess, holding a shaving-knife in the hand; and the Red Makara-Headed Peaceful-Goddess, holding an urn in the hand; and the Red Scorpion-Headed Amṛitā-Goddess, holding a lotus in the hand; and the White Kite-Headed Moon-Goddess, holding a *dorje* in the hand; and the Dark-Green Fox-Headed Baton-Goddess, flourishing a club in the hand; and the Yellowish-Black Tiger-Headed Rākṣhasī, holding a blood-filled skull-bowl in the hand: [these] the Six Yoginīs of the South, issuing from within the [southern quarter of thine own] brain, will come to shine upon thee; fear that not.

O nobly-born, from the west [will dawn] the Greenish-Black Vulture-Headed Eater-Goddess, holding a baton in the hand; and the Red Horse-Headed Delight-Goddess, holding a huge trunk of a corpse; and the White Eagle-Headed Mighty-Goddess, holding a club in the hand; and the Yellow Dog-Headed Rākṣhasī, holding a *dorje* in the hand and a shaving-knife and cutting [with this]; and the Red Hoopoo-Headed Desire-Goddess, holding a bow and arrow in the hand aimed; and the Green Stag-Headed Wealth-Guardian Goddess, holding an urn in the hand: [these], the Six Yoginīs of the West, issuing from within the [western quarter of thine own] brain, will come to shine upon thee; fear that not.

O nobly-born, from the north [will dawn] the Blue Wolf-Headed Wind-Goddess, waving a pennant in the hand; and the Red Ibex-

Headed Woman-Goddess, holding a pointed stake in the hand; and the Black Sow-Headed Sow-Goddess, holding a noose of fangs in the hand; and the Red Crow-Headed Thunderbolt-Goddess, holding an infant corpse in the hand; and the Greenish-Black Elephant-Headed Big-Nosed Goddess, holding in the hand a big corpse and drinking blood from a skull; and the Blue Serpent-Headed Water-Goddess, holding in the hand a serpent noose: [these], the Six Yoginīs of the North, issuing from within [the northern quarter of] thine own brain, will come to shine upon thee; fear that not.

O nobly-born, the Four Yoginīs of the Door, issuing from within the brain, will come to shine upon thee: from the east, the Black Cuckoo-Headed Mystic Goddess, holding an iron hook in the hand; from the south, the Yellow Goat-Headed Mystic Goddess, holding a noose in the hand; from the west, the Red Lion-Headed Mystic Goddess, holding an iron chain in the hand; and from the north, the Greenish-Black Serpent-Headed Mystic Goddess: [these], the Four Door-Keeping Yoginīs, issuing from within the brain, will come to shine upon thee.

Since these Twenty-eight Mighty Goddesses emanate from the bodily powers of Ratna-Sambhava, [He] of the Six Heruka Deities, recognize them.

O nobly-born, the Peaceful Deities emanate from the Voidness of the *Dharma-Kāya*;[52] recognize them. From the Radiance of the *Dharma-Kāya*[53] emanate the Wrathful Deities; recognize them.

At this time when the Fifty-eight Blood-Drinking Deities emanating from thine own brain come to shine upon thee, if thou knowest them to be the radiances of thine own intellect, thou wilt

---

52 Emanations from the void, or innate, unshaped aspects of the *Darma-Kāya* state, viewing man as the microcosm of the macrocosm.

53 Emanations from the active radiant aspect of the *Darma-Kāya* state – man as the microcosm of the macrocosm being inseparable.

merge, in the state of at-one-ment, into the body of the Blood-Drinking Ones there and then, and obtain Buddhahood.

O nobly-born, by not recognizing now, and by fleeing from the deities out of fear, again sufferings will come to overpower thee. If this be not known, fear being begotten of the Blood-Drinking Deities, [one is] awed and terrified and fainteth away: one's own thought-forms turn into illusory appearances, and one wandereth into the *Sangsāra*; if one be not awed and terrified, one will not wander into the *Sangsāra*.

Furthermore, the bodies of the largest of the Peaceful and Wrathful Deities are equal [in vastness] to the limits of the heavens; the intermediate, as big as Mt Meru;[54] the smallest, equal to eighteen bodies such as thine own body, set one upon another. Be not terrified at that; be not awed. If all existing phenomena shining forth as divine shapes and radiances be recognized to be the emanations of one's own intellect, Buddhahood will be obtained at that very instant of recognition. The saying, 'Buddhahood will be obtained in a moment [of time]' is that which applieth now. Bearing this in mind, one will obtain Buddhahood by merging, in at-one-ment, into the Radiances and the *Kāyas*.

O nobly-born, whatever fearful and terrifying visions thou mayst see, recognize them to be thine own thought-forms.

O nobly-born, if thou recognize not, and be frightened, then all the Peaceful Deities will shine forth in the shape of Mahā-Kāla;[55] and all the Wrathful Deities will shine [forth] in the form of Dharma-Rāja, the Lord of Death;[56] and thine own thought-forms becoming Illusions [or *Māras*], thou wilt wander into the *Sangsāra*.

O nobly-born, if one recognize not one's own thought-forms,

54 Mt Meru is the central mystical mountain of Buddhist cosmography.

55 At this stage all unreal forms of the Peaceful Deities merge and appear as this one deity.

56 This illusory deity assumes many forms which can blend into a single form.

however learned one may be in the Scriptures – both *Sūtras* and *Tantras* – although practising religion for a *kalpa*, one obtaineth not Buddhahood. If one recognize one's own thought-forms, by one important art and by one word, Buddhahood is obtained.

If one's thought-forms be not recognized as soon as one dieth, the shapes of Dharma-Rāja, the Lord of Death, will shine forth on the *Chönyid-Bardo*. The largest of the bodies of Dharma-Rāja, the Lord of Death, equalling the heavens [in vastness]; the intermediate, Mt Meru; the smallest, eighteen times one's own body, will come filling the world-systems. They will come having their upper teeth biting the nether lip; their eyes glassy; their hair tied up on the top of the head; big-bellied, narrow-waisted; holding a [*karmic*] record-board[57] in the hand; giving utterance from their mouth to sounds of 'Strike! Slay!', licking [human] brain, drinking blood, tearing heads from corpses, tearing out [the] hearts: thus will [they] come, filling the worlds.

O nobly-born, when such thought-forms emanate, be thou not afraid, nor terrified; the body which now thou possessest being a mental-body of [*karmic*] propensities, though slain and chopped [to bits], cannot die. Because thy body is, in reality, one of voidness, thou needest not fear. The [bodies of the] Lord of Death, too, are emanations from the radiances of thine own intellect; they are not constituted of matter; voidness cannot injure voidness. Beyond the emanations of thine own intellectual faculties, externally, the Peaceful and the Wrathful Ones, the Blood-Drinking Ones, the Various-Headed Ones, the rainbow lights, the terrifying forms of the Lord of Death, exist not in reality: of this, there is no doubt. Thus, knowing this, all the fear and terror is self-dissipated; and, merging in the state of at-one-ment, Buddhahood is obtained.

If thou recognizest in that manner, exerting thy faith and affec-

---

57 A board inscribed with *karmic* records of the life of the deceased.

tion towards the tutelary deities and believing that they have come
to receive thee amidst the ambuscades of the *Bardo*, think, '[I] take
refuge [in them]'; and remember the Precious Trinity, exerting
towards them [the Trinity] fondness and faith. Whosoever thine
own tutelary deity may be, recollect now; [and] calling him by
name, pray thus:

'[Alas!] Wandering am I in the *Bardo*; run to my rescue;
Uphold me by thy grace, O Precious Tutelary!'
Calling upon the name of thine own *guru*, pray thus:
'[Alas!] Wandering am I in the *Bardo*; rescue me!
[O] let not thy grace forsake me!'

Have faith in the Blood-Drinking Deities, too, and offer up this
prayer:

'Alas! When [I am] wandering in the *Sangsāra*, through
    force of overpowering illusions,
On the light-path of the abandonment of fright, fear, and
    awe,
May the bands of the Bhagavāns, the Peaceful and Wrathful
    Ones, lead [me],
May the bands of the Wrathful Goddess Rich in Space be
    [my] rear-guard,
And save me from the fearful ambuscades of the *Bardo*,
And place me in the state of the Perfectly-Enlightened
    Buddhas.
When wandering alone, separated from dear friends,
When the void forms of one's own thoughts are shining
    here,
May the Buddhas, exerting the force of their grace,
Cause not to come the fear, awe, and terror in the *Bardo*.

When the five bright Wisdom-Lights are shining here,
May recognition come without dread and without awe;
When the divine bodies of the Peaceful and the Wrathful
    are shining here;
May the assurance of fearlessness be obtained and the *Bardo*
    be recognized.
When, by the power of evil *karma*, misery is being tasted,
May the tutelary deities dissipate the misery;
When the natural sound of Reality is reverberating [like]
    a thousand thunders,
May they be transmuted into the sounds of the Six Syllables.[58]
When unprotected, *karma* having to be followed here,
I beseech the Gracious Compassionate [One][59] to protect
    me;
When suffering miseries of *karmic* propensities here,
May the blissfulness of the Clear Light dawn;
May the Five Elements[60] not rise up as enemies;
But may I behold the realms of the Five Orders of the
    Enlightened Ones.'

Thus, in earnest faith and humility, offer up the prayer; whereby all fears will vanish and Buddhahood in the *Sambhoga-Kāya* will undoubtedly be won: important is this. Being undistracted, repeat it in that manner, three or [even] seven times.

However heavy the evil *karma* may be and however weak the remaining karma may be, it is not possible that liberation will not be obtained [if one but recognize]. If, nevertheless, despite

58 The *mantra* of Chenrazee, the patron-god of Tibet. Its repetition in the human world and on the *Bardo*-plane is credited with terminating the cycle of rebirth, thus allowing entry into Nirvāṇa.

59 Chenrazee.

60 Earth, Air, Water, Fire, Ether.

everything done in these [stages of the *Bardo*], recognition is still not brought about, then – there being danger of one's wandering further, into the third *Bardo*, called the *Sidpa Bardo* – the setting-face-to-face for that will be shown in detail hereinafter.

THE CONCLUSION, SHOWING THE FUNDAMENTAL IMPORTANCE OF THE BARDO TEACHINGS

Whatever the religious practices of any one may have been – whether extensive or limited – during the moments of death various misleading illusions occur; and hence this *Thödol* is indispensable. To those who have meditated much, the real Truth dawneth as soon as the body and consciousness-principle part. The acquiring of experience while living is important: they who have [then] recognized [the true nature of] their own being, and thus have had some experience, obtain great power during the *Bardo* of the Moments of Death, when the Clear Light dawneth.

Again, the meditation on the deities of the Mystic Path of the *Mantra*, [both in the] visualizing and the perfecting stages, while living, will be of great influence when the peaceful and wrathful visions dawn on the *Chönyid Bardo*. Thus the training in this *Bardo* being of particular importance even while living, hold to it, read it, commit it to memory, bear it in mind properly, read it regularly thrice; let the words and the meanings be very clear; it should be so that the words and the meanings will not be forgotten even though a hundred executioners were pursuing [thee].

It is called the Great Liberation by Hearing, because even those who have committed the five boundless sins[61] are sure to be liberated if they hear it by the path of the ear. Therefore read it in the midst of vast congregations. Disseminate it. Through having heard it once, even though one do not comprehend it, it will be remem-

---

61 Patricide, matricide, setting two religious bodies at war, killing a saint and causing blood to flow from the body of a Tathāgata.

bered in the Intermediate State without a word being omitted, for the intellect becometh ninefold more lucid [there]. Hence it should be proclaimed in the ears of all living persons; it should be read over the pillows of all persons who are ill; it should be read at the side of all corpses: it should be spread broadcast.

Those who meet with this [doctrine] are indeed fortunate. Save for them who have accumulated much merit and absolved many obscurations, difficult is it to meet with it. Even when met with, difficult is it to comprehend it. Liberation will be won through simply not disbelieving it upon hearing it. Therefore treat this [doctrine] very dearly: it is the essence of all doctrines.

The Setting-Face-to-Face while experiencing Reality in the Intermediate State, called 'The Teaching Which Liberateth By Merely Being Heard And That Which Liberateth By Merely Being Attached',[62] is finished.

62 The *Thadol*.

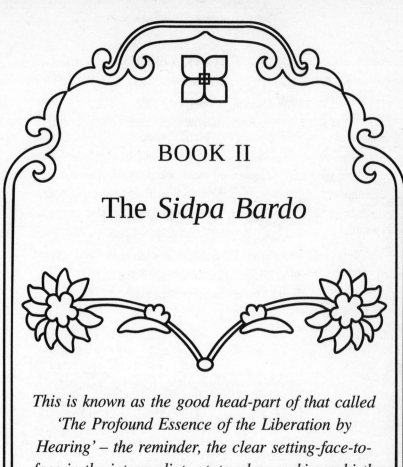

BOOK II

The *Sidpa Bardo*

This is known as the good head-part of that called 'The Profound Essence of the Liberation by Hearing' – the reminder, the clear setting-face-to-face in the intermediate state when seeking rebirth

'The essence of all things is one and the same, perfectly calm and tranquil, and shows no sign of "becoming"; ignorance, however, is in its blindness and delusion oblivious of Enlightenment, and, on that account, cannot recognize truthfully all those conditions, differences, and activities which characterize the phenomena of the Universe.'
– Ashvaghosha

THE OBEISANCES

To the assembled Deities, to the Tutelaries, to the *Gurus*,
Humbly is obeisance paid:
May Liberation in the Intermediate State be vouchsafed
by Them.

INTRODUCTORY VERSES

'Above, in the Great *Bardo-Thödol*,
The *Bardo* called *Chönyid* was taught;
And now, of the *Bardo* called *Sidpa*,
The vivid reminder is brought.'

PART I

The After-Death World

Introductory Instructions to the Officiant: Although, heretofore, while in the *Chönyid Bardo*, many vivid remindings have been given – setting aside those who have had great familiarity with the real Truth and those who have good *karma* – for them of evil *karma* who have had no familiarity, and for them of evil *karma* who because of the influence thereof become stricken with fear and terror, recognition is difficult. These go down to the Fourteenth Day; and, to reimpress them vividly, that which follows is to be read.

THE BARDO BODY: ITS BIRTH AND ITS SUPERNORMAL FACULTIES

Worship having been offered to the Trinity, and the prayer invoking the aid of the Buddhas and Bodhisattvas having been recited, then, calling the deceased by name, three or seven times, speak thus:

O nobly-born, listen thou well, and bear at heart that birth in the Hell-world, in the *Deva*-world, and in this *Bardo*-body is of the kind called supernormal birth.

Indeed, when thou wert experiencing the radiances of the

Peaceful and the Wrathful, in the *Chönyid Bardo*, being unable to recognize, thou didst faint away, through fear, about three and one-half days [after thy decease]; and, then, when thou wert recovered from the swoon, thy Knower must have risen up in its primordial condition and a radiant body, resembling the former body, must have sprung forth[1] – as the *Tantra* says:

> 'Having a body [seemingly] fleshly [resembling]
>   the former and that to be produced,
> Endowed with all sense-faculties and power of
>   unimpeded motion,
> Possessing *karmic* miraculous powers,
> Visible to pure celestial eyes [of *Bardo* beings]
>   of like nature.'

Such, then, is the teaching.

That [radiant body] – thus referred to as [resembling] 'the former and that to be produced' (meaning that one will have a body just like the body of flesh and blood, the former human, propensity body) – will also be endowed with certain signs and beauties of perfection such as beings of high destiny possess.

This body, [born] of desire, is a thought-form hallucination in the Intermediate State, and it is called desire-body.

At that time – if thou art to be born as a *deva* – visions of the *Deva*-world will appear to thee; similarly – wherever thou art to be born – if as an asura, or a human being, or a brute, or a *preta*, or a being in Hell, a vision of the place will appear to thee.

Accordingly, the word 'former' [in the quotation] implieth that prior to the three-and-one-half days thou wilt have been thinking

---

1   About three and a half days after death the *Bardo*-body is said to spring forth instantaneously.

thou hadst the same sort of a body as the former body of flesh and blood, possessed by thee in the former existence because of habitual propensities; and the word 'produced' is so used because, afterwards, the vision of thy future place of birth will appear to thee. Hence, the expression as a whole, 'former and that to be produced', referreth to these [i.e. the fleshly body just discarded and the fleshly body to be assumed at rebirth].

At that time, follow not the visions which appear to thee. Be not attracted; be not weak: if, through weakness, thou be fond of them, thou wilt have to wander amidst the Six *Lokas* and suffer pain.

Up to the other day thou wert unable to recognize the *Chönyid Bardo* and hast had to wander down this far. Now, if thou art to hold fast to the real Truth, thou must allow thy mind to rest undistractedly in the nothing-to-do, nothing-to-hold condition of the unobscured, primordial, bright, void state of thine intellect, to which thou hast been introduced by thy *guru*. [Thereby] thou wilt obtain Liberation without having to enter the door of the womb. But if thou art unable to know thyself, then, whosoever may be thy tutelary deity and thy *guru*, meditate on them, in a state of intense fondness and humble trust, as overshadowing the crown of thy head.[2] This is of great importance. Be not distracted.

Instructions to the Officiant: thus speak, and, if recognition result from that, Liberation will be obtained, without need of the wandering in the Six *Lokas*. If, however, through influence of bad *karma*, recognition is made difficult, thereupon say as follows:

O nobly-born, again listen. 'Endowed with all sense-faculties and power of unimpeded motion' implieth [that although] thou mayst have been, when living, blind of the eye, or deaf, or lame,

---

2 The Brāhmanic Aperture, through which the consciousness-principle leaves the body, is located on the crown of the head. As a result, if the visualization is centred there it will be very beneficial.

yet on this After-Death Plane thine eyes will see forms, and thine ears will hear sounds, and all other sense-organs of thine will be unimpaired and very keen and complete. Wherefore the *Bardo*-body hath been spoken of as 'endowed with all sense-faculties'. That [condition of existence, in which thou thyself now art] is an indication that thou art deceased and wandering in the *Bardo*. Act so as to know this. Remember the teachings; remember the teachings.

O nobly-born, 'unimpeded motion' implieth that thy present body being a desire-body – thine intellect having been separated from its seat[3] – is not a body of gross matter, so that now thou hast the power to go right through any rock-masses, hills, boulders, earth, houses, and Mt Meru itself without being impeded. Excepting Budh-Gayā and the mother's womb, even the King of Mountains, Mt Meru itself, can be passed through by thee, straight forwards and backwards unimpededly. That, too, is an indication that thou art wandering in the *Sidpa Bardo*. Remember thy *guru's* teachings, and pray to the Compassionate Lord.

O nobly-born, thou art actually endowed with the power of miraculous action,[4] which is not, however, the fruit of any *samādhi*, but a power come to thee naturally; and, therefore, it is of the nature of *karmic* power. Thou art able in a moment to traverse the four continents round about Mt Meru. Or thou canst instantaneously arrive in whatever place thou wishest; thou hast the power of reaching there within the time which a man taketh to bend, or to stretch forth his hand. These various powers of illusion and of shape-shifting desire not, desire not.

None is there [of such powers] which thou mayest desire which thou canst not exhibit. The ability to exercise them unimpededly existeth in thee now. Know this, and pray to the *guru*.

---

3 The human body that has been left behind after death.

4 Power to change one's shape or to appear or disappear at will. It can be developed on earth through the practice of *yoga*.

O nobly-born, 'Visible to pure celestial eyes of like nature' implieth that those [beings] of like nature, being those of similar constitution [or level of knowledge] in the Intermediate State, will individually see each other.[5] For example, those beings who are destined to be born amongst *devas* will see each other [and so on]. Dote not on them [seen by thee], but meditate upon the Compassionate One.

'Visible to pure celestial eyes' [also] implieth that the *devas*, being born [pure] in virtue of merit, are visible to the pure celestial eyes of those who practise *dhyāna*. These will not see them at all times; when mentally concentrated [upon them] they see [them], when not, they see [them] not. Sometimes, even when practising *dhyāna*, they are liable to become distracted [and not see them].

CHARACTERISTICS OF EXISTENCE IN THE INTERMEDIATE STATE

O nobly-born, the possessor of that sort of body will see places [familiarly known on the earth-plane] and relatives [there] as one seeth another in dreams.

Thou seest thy relatives and connections and speakest to them, but receivest no reply. Then, seeing them and thy family weeping, thou thinkest, 'I am dead! What shall I do?' and feelest great misery, just like a fish cast out [of water] on red-hot embers. Such misery thou wilt be experiencing at present. But feeling miserable will avail thee nothing now. If thou hast a divine *guru*,[6] pray to him. Pray to the Tutelary Deity, the Compassionate One. Even though thou feelest attachment for thy relatives and connections, it will do thee no good. So be not attached. Pray to the Compassionate Lord; thou shalt have nought of sorrow, or of terror, or of awe.

---

5   *Lāmas* believe that there are five kinds of eyes, apart from the normal human eyes: Eyes of Instinct, Celestial Eyes, Eyes of Truth, Divine Eyes and Eyes of Wisdom of the Buddhas. All five types have capabilities far beyond those of normal human eyes.

6   A superhuman *guru* of the Divyaugha Order.

O nobly-born, when thou art driven [hither and thither] by the ever-moving wind of *karma*, thine intellect, having no object upon which to rest, will be like a feather tossed about by the wind, riding on the horse of breath. Ceaselessly and involuntarily wilt thou be wandering about. To all those who are weeping [thou wilt say], 'Here I am; weep not.' But they not hearing thee, thou wilt think, 'I am dead!' And again, at that time, thou wilt be feeling very miserable. Be not miserable in that way.

There will be a grey twilight-like light, both by night and by day, and at all times.[7] In that kind of Intermediate State thou wilt be either for one, two, three, four, five, six, or seven weeks, until the forty-ninth day. It hath been said that ordinarily the miseries of the *Sidpa Bardo* are experienced for about twenty-two days; but, because of the determining influence of *karma*, a fixed period is not assured.

O nobly-born, at about that time, the fierce wind of *karma*, terrific and hard to endure, will drive thee [onwards], from behind, in dreadful gusts. Fear it not. That is thine own illusion. Thick awesome darkness will appear in front of thee continually, from the midst of which there will come such terror-producing utterances as 'Strike! Slay!' and similar threats.[8] Fear these not.

In other cases, of persons of much evil *karma*, *karmically*-produced flesh-eating *rākṣhasas* [or demons] bearing various weapons will utter, 'Strike! Slay!' and so on, making a frightful tumult. They will come upon one as if competing amongst themselves as to which [of them] should get hold of one. Apparitional illusions, too, of being pursued by various terrible beasts of prey will dawn. Snow, rain, darkness, fierce blasts [of wind], and hallucinations of being

7   The light of the sun, moon and stars is not visible to the deceased in the *Bardo*-body. Only natural light, the 'astral light', is seen after death. This light is diffused through the ether, in much the same way as natural light is diffused at twilight.

8   The *Bardo* dweller is consumed by the belief that the other *Bardo* dwellers are his enemies. This is because of the *karmic* effects of selfishness in the human world.

pursued by many people likewise will come; [and] sounds as of mountains crumbling down, and of angry overflowing seas, and of the roaring of fire, and of fierce winds springing up.

When these sounds come one, being terrified by them, will flee before them in every direction, not caring whither one fleeth. But the way will be obstructed by three awful precipices – white, and black, and red. They will be terror-inspiring and deep, and one will feel as if one were about to fall down them. O nobly-born, they are not really precipices; they are Anger, Lust and Stupidity.[9]

Know at that time that it is the *Sidpa Bardo* [in which thou art]. Invoking, by name, the Compassionate One, pray earnestly, thus: 'O Compassionate Lord, and my *Guru*, and the Precious Trinity, suffer it not that I (so-and-so by name) fall into the unhappy worlds.' Act so as to forget this not.

Others who have accumulated merit, and devoted themselves sincerely to religion, will experience various delightful pleasures and happiness and ease in full measure. But that class of neutral beings who have neither earned merit nor created bad *karma* will experience neither pleasure nor pain, but a sort of colourless stupidity of indifference. O nobly-born, whatever cometh in that manner – whatever delightful pleasures thou mayst experience – be not attracted by them; dote not [on them]: think, 'May the *Guru* and the Trinity be worshipped [with these merit-given delights].' Abandon all dotings and hankerings.

Even though thou dost not experience pleasure, or pain, but only indifference, keep thine intellect in the undistracted state of the [meditation upon the] Great Symbol, without thinking that thou art meditating. This is of vast importance.[10]

---

9   The precipices are *karmic* illusions. Falling into them symbolizes the entry into a womb before rebirth.

10 This state of mental concentration in which no thought of meditation is allowed to intrude is the state of *Samādhi*. The act of thinking about meditating itself prevents the meditation.

O nobly-born, at that time, at bridge-heads, in temples, by *stūpas* of eight kinds,[11] thou wilt rest a little while, but thou wilt not be able to remain there very long, for thine intellect hath been separated from thine [earth-plane] body. Because of this inability to loiter, thou oft-times wilt feel perturbed and vexed and panic-stricken. At times, thy Knower will be dim; at times, fleeting and incoherent. Thereupon this thought will occur to thee, 'Alas! I am dead! What shall I do?' And because of such thought the Knower will become saddened and the heart chilled, and thou wilt experience infinite misery of sorrow.[12] Since thou canst not rest in any one place, and feel impelled to go on, think not of various things, but allow the intellect to abide in its own [unmodified] state.

As to food, only that which hath been dedicated to thee can be partaken of by thee, and no other food.[13] As to friends at this time, there will be no certainty.

These are the indications of the wandering about on the *Sidpa Bardo* of the mental-body. At the time, happiness and misery will depend upon *karma*. Thou wilt see thine own home, the attendants, relatives, and the corpse, and think, 'Now I am dead! What shall I do?' And being oppressed with intense sorrow, the thought will occur to thee, 'O what would I not give to possess a body!' And so thinking, thou wilt be wandering hither and thither seeking a body.

Even though thou couldst enter thy dead body nine times over – owing to the long interval which thou hast passed in the *Chönyid*

---

11 The eight purposes for which a *stūpa* (or pagoda) is built. Some of them are: marking a victory; marking the spot where a saint died; enshrining sacred books or relics, or purely as an object of worship.

12 All of the problems met by the deceased in the *Bardo* are *karmic*. Had he been developed spiritually he would have had a happy, and shorter, *Bardo* existence.

13 The dwellers in the *Bardo* are said to live on invisible ethereal essences which they extract from either food presented to them on the human plane or from the general storehouse of nature.

Bardo – it will have been frozen if in winter, been decomposed if in summer, or, otherwise, thy relatives will have cremated it, or interred it, or thrown it into the water, or given it to the birds and beasts of prey.[14] Wherefore finding no place for thyself to enter into, thou wilt be dissatisfied and have the sensation of being squeezed into cracks and crevices amidst rocks and boulders.[15] The experiencing of this sort of misery occurs in the Intermediate State when seeking rebirth. Even though thou seekest a body, thou wilt gain nothing but trouble. Put aside the desire for a body; and permit thy mind to abide in the state of resignation, and act so as to abide therein.

By thus being set-face-to-face, one obtaineth liberation from the *Bardo*.

THE JUDGEMENT

Instructions to the Officiant: Yet, again, it may be possible that because of the influence of bad *karma* one will not recognize even thus. Therefore, call the deceased by name, and speak as follows:

O nobly-born, (so-and-so), listen. That thou art suffering so cometh from thine own *karma*; it is not due to any one else's: it is by thine own *karma*. Accordingly, pray earnestly to the Precious Trinity; that will protect thee.

If thou neither prayest nor knowest how to meditate upon the Great Symbol nor upon any tutelary deity, the Good Genius,[16] who was born simultaneously with thee, will come now and count out thy good deeds [with] white pebbles, and the Evil Genius,[17] who was born simultaneously with thee, will come and count out thy

---

14 All known forms of corpse disposal are carried out in Tibet.

15 This represents the act of getting into undesirable wombs, like those of human beings with an animal-like nature.

16 The personification of a human's higher, or divine, nature.

17 The personification of a human's lower, or carnal, nature.

evil deeds [with] black pebbles. Thereupon, thou wilt be greatly frightened, awed, and terrified, and wilt tremble; and thou wilt attempt to tell lies, saying, 'I have not committed any evil deed.'

Then the Lord of Death will say, 'I will consult the Mirror of *Karma*.'

So saying, he will look in the Mirror, wherein every good and evil act is vividly reflected. Lying will be of no avail.

Then [one of the Executive Furies of] the Lord of Death will place round thy neck a rope and drag thee along; he will cut off thy head, extract thy heart, pull out thy intestines, lick up thy brain, drink thy blood, eat thy flesh, and gnaw thy bones;[18] but thou wilt be incapable of dying. Although thy body be hacked to pieces, it will revive again. The repeated hacking will cause intense pain and torture.

Even at the time that the pebbles are being counted out, be not frightened, nor terrified; tell no lies; and fear not the Lord of Death.

Thy body being a mental body is incapable of dying even though beheaded and quartered. In reality, thy body is of the nature of voidness; thou needst not be afraid. The Lords of Death are thine own hallucinations.[19] Thy desire-body is a body of propensities, and void. Voidness cannot injure voidness; the qualityless cannot injure the qualityless.

Apart from one's own hallucinations, in reality there are no such things existing outside oneself as Lord of Death, or god, or demon, or the Bull-headed Spirit of Death. Act so as to recognize this.

At this time, act so as to recognize that thou art in the *Bardo*. Meditate upon the *Samādhi* of the Great Symbol. If thou dost not know how to meditate, then merely analyse with care the real nature

18 These tortures symbolize the guilty twinges of the conscience of the deceased – the Mirror is memory.

19 These Lords of Death are Yama-Rāja and his Court of Associates, perhaps including the Executive Furies.

of that which is frightening thee. In reality it is not formed into anything, but is a Voidness which is the *Dharma-Kāya*.

That Voidness is not of the nature of the voidness of nothingness, but a Voidness at the true nature of which thou feelest awed, and before which thine intellect shineth clearly and more lucidly; that is the [state of] mind of the *Sambhoga-Kāya*.

In that state wherein thou art existing, there is being experienced by thee, in an unbearable intensity, voidness and Brightness inseparable – the Voidness bright by nature and the Brightness by nature void, and the Brightness inseparable from the Voidness – a state of the primordial [or unmodified] intellect, which is the *Ādi-Kāya*.[20] And the power of this, shining unobstructedly, will radiate everywhere; it is the *Nirmāṇa-Kāya*.

O nobly-born, listen unto me undistractedly. By merely recognizing the Four Kāyas, thou art certain to obtain perfect Emancipation in any of Them. Be not distracted. The line of demarcation between Buddhas and sentient beings lieth herein.[21] This moment is one of great importance; if thou shouldst be distracted now, it will require innumerable aeons of time for thee to come out of the Quagmire of Misery.

A saying, the truth of which is applicable, is:

'In a moment of time, a marked differentiation is
    created;
In a moment of time, Perfect Enlightenment is
    obtained.'

Till the moment which hath just passed, all this *Bardo* hath been dawning upon thee and yet thou hast not recognized, because of

20 Or 'First Body', which is synonymous with the *Darma-Kāya*.

21 Buddhas are aware of the true nature of *sangsāric* existence – which is that all phenomena are merely illusory

being distracted. On this account, thou hast experienced all the fear and terror. Shouldst thou become distracted now, the chords of divine compassion of the Compassionate Eyes will break, and thou wilt go into the place from which there is no [immediate] liberation. Therefore, be careful. Even though thou hast not recognized ere this – despite thus being set-face-to-face – thou wilt recognize and obtain liberation here.

Instructions to the Officiant: if it be an illiterate boor who knoweth not how to meditate, then say this:

O nobly-born, if thou knowest not how thus to meditate, act so as to remember the Compassionate One, and the Saṅgha, the Dharma, and the Buddha, and pray. Think of all these fears and terrifying apparitions as being thine own tutelary deity, or as the Compassionate One. Bring to thy recollection the mystic name that hath been given thee at the time of thy sacred initiation when thou wert a human being, and the name of thy guru, and tell them to the Righteous King of the Lord[s] of Death. Even though thou fallest down precipices, thou wilt not be hurt. Avoid awe and terror.

THE ALL-DETERMINING INFLUENCE OF THOUGHT

Instructions to the Officiant: Say that; for by such setting-face-to-face, despite the previous non-liberation, liberation ought surely to be obtained here. Possibly, [however,] liberation may not be obtained even after that setting-face-to-face; and earnest and continued application being essential, again calling the deceased by name, speak as follows:

O nobly-born, thy immediate experiences will be of momentary joys followed by momentary sorrows, of great intensity, like the [taut and relaxed] mechanical actions of catapults. Be not in the least attached [to the joys] nor displeased [by the sorrows] of that.

If thou art to be born on a higher plane, the vision of that higher plane will be dawning upon thee.

Thy living relatives may – by way of dedication for the benefit of thee deceased – be sacrificing many animals, and performing religious ceremonies, and giving alms. Thou, because of thy vision not being purified, mayst be inclined to grow very angry at their actions and bring about, at this moment, thy birth in Hell:[22] whatever those left behind thee may be doing, act thou so that no angry thought can arise in thee, and meditate upon love for them.

Furthermore, even if thou feelest attached to the worldly goods thou hast left behind, or, because of seeing such worldly goods of thine in the possession of other people and being enjoyed by them, thou shouldst feel attached to them through weakness, or feel angry with thy successors, that feeling will affect the psychological moment in such a way that, even though thou wert destined to be born on higher and happier planes, thou wilt be obliged to be born in Hell, or in the world of *pretas* [or unhappy ghosts]. On the other hand, even if thou art attached to worldly goods left behind, thou wilt not be able to possess them, and they will be of no use to thee. Therefore, abandon weakness and attachment for them; cast them away wholly; renounce them from thy heart. No matter who may be enjoying thy worldly goods, have no feeling of miserliness, but be prepared to renounce them willingly. Think that thou art offering them to the Precious Trinity and to thy *guru*, and abide in the feeling of unattachment, devoid of weakness [of desire].

Again, when any recitation of the *Kamkanī Mantra*[23] is being made on thy behalf as a funeral rite, or when any rite for the absolving of bad *karma* liable to bring about thy birth in lower regions is being

22 When an animal is sacrificed, the deceased is unable to escape the *karmic* result and horrors are immediately inflicted upon him. But if he gets angry because of it he is forced down to the lowest mental state, which is Hell.

23 This *mantra* is believed to have the magical power of transforming food left as offerings for the dead.

performed for thee, the sight of their being conducted in an incorrect way, mixed up with sleep and distraction and non-observance of the vows and lack of purity [on the part of any officiant], and such things indicating levity – all of which thou wilt be able to see because thou art endowed with limited *karmic* power of prescience – thou mayst feel lack of faith and entire disbelief [in thy religion]. Thou wilt be able to apprehend any fear and fright, any black actions, irreligious conduct, and incorrectly recited rituals. In thy mind thou mayst think, 'Alas! They are, indeed, playing me false.' Thinking thus, thou wilt be extremely depressed, and, through great resentment, thou wilt acquire disbelief and loss of faith, instead of affection and humble trustfulness. This affecting the psychological moment, thou wilt be certain to be born in one of the miserable states.

Such [thought] will not only be of no use to thee, but will do thee great harm. However incorrect the ritual and improper the conduct of the priests performing thy funeral rites, [think], 'What! Mine own thoughts must be impure! How can it be possible that the words of the Buddha should be incorrect? It is like the reflection of the blemishes on mine own face which I see in a mirror; mine own thoughts must [indeed] be impure. As for these [i.e. the priests], the Saṅgha is their body, the Dharma their utterance, and in their mind they are the Buddha in reality: I will take refuge in them.'

Thus thinking, put thy trust in them and exercise sincere love towards them. Then whatever is done for thee [by those] left behind will truly tend to thy benefit. Therefore the exercise of that love is of much importance; do not forget this.

Again, even if thou wert to be born in one of the miserable states and the light of that miserable state shone upon thee, yet by thy successors and relatives performing white[24] religious rites unmixed with evil actions, and the abbots and learned priests

24 As opposed to black, as in black magic.

devoting themselves, body, speech, and mind, to the performance of the correct meritorious rituals, the delight from thy feeling greatly cheered at seeing them will, by its own virtue, so affect the psychological moment that, even though thou deservest a birth in the unhappy states, there will be brought about thy birth on a higher and happier plane. [Therefore] thou shouldst not create impious thoughts, but exercise pure affection and humble faith towards all impartially. This is highly important. Hence be extremely careful.

O nobly-born, to sum up: thy present intellect in the Intermediate State having no firm object whereon to depend, being of little weight and continuously in motion, whatever thought occurs to thee now – be it pious or impious – will wield great power; therefore think not in thy mind of impious things, but recall any devotional exercises; or, if thou wert unaccustomed to any such exercises, [show forth] pure affection and humble faith; pray to the Compassionate One, or to thy tutelary deities; with full resolve, utter this prayer:

> 'Alas! While wandering alone, separated from
>   loving friends,
> When the vacuous, reflected body of mine own
>   mental ideas dawneth upon me,
> May the Buddhas, vouchsafing their power of
>   compassion,
> Grant that there shall be no fear, awe, or terror
>   in the *Bardo*.
> When experiencing miseries, through the power
>   of evil *karma*,
> May the tutelary deities dispel the miseries.
> When the thousand thunders of the Sound of
>   Reality reverberate,
> May they all be sounds of the Six Syllables.

> When *Karma* follows, without there being any
>   protector,
> May the Compassionate One protect me, I pray.
> When experiencing the sorrows of *karmic* propen-
>   sities here,
> May the radiance of the happy clear light of
>   *Samādhi* shine upon me.'

Earnest prayer in this form will be sure to guide thee along; thou mayst rest assured that thou wilt not be deceived. Of great importance is this: through that being recited, again recollection cometh; and recognition and liberation will be achieved.

THE DAWNING OF THE LIGHTS OF THE SIX LOKAS

Instructions to the Officiant: Yet – though this [instruction] be so oft repeated – if recognition be difficult, because of the influence of evil *karma*, much benefit will come from repeating these settings-face-to-face many times over. Once more, [then,] call the deceased by name, and speak as follows:

O nobly-born, if thou hast been unable to apprehend the above, henceforth the body of the past life will become more and more dim and the body of the future life will become more and more clear. Saddened at this [thou wilt think], 'O what misery I am undergoing! Now, whatever body I am to get, I shall go and seek [it].' So thinking, thou wilt be going hither and thither, ceaselessly and distractedly. Then there will shine upon thee the lights of the Six *Sangsāric Lokas*. The light of that place wherein thou art to be born, through power of karma, will shine most prominently.

O nobly-born, listen. If thou desirest to know what those six lights are: there will shine upon thee a dull white light from the *Deva*-world, a dull green light from the *Asura*-world, a dull yellow light from the Human-world, a dull blue light from the Brute-world, a dull red light from the *Preta*-world, and a smoke-coloured light from the Hell-world. At that time, by the power of *karma*, thine own body will partake of the colour of the light of the place wherein thou art to be born.

O nobly-born, the special art of these teachings is especially important at this moment: whichever light shineth upon thee now, meditate upon it as being the Compassionate One; from whatever place the light cometh, consider that [place] to be [or to exist in] the Compassionate One. This is an exceedingly profound art; it will prevent birth. Or whosoever thy tutelary deity may be, meditate upon the form for much time – as being apparent yet non-existent in reality, like a form produced by a magician. That is called the pure illusory form. Then let the [visualization of the] tutelary deity melt away from the extremities, till nothing at all remaineth visible of it; and put thyself in the state of the Clearness and the Voidness – which thou canst not conceive as something – and abide in that state for a little while. Again meditate upon the tutelary deity; again meditate upon the Clear Light: do this alternately. Afterwards, allow thine own intellect also to melt away gradually,[25] [beginning] from the extremities.

Wherever the ether pervadeth, consciousness pervadeth; wherever consciousness pervadeth, the *Dharma-Kāya* pervadeth. Abide tranquilly in the uncreated state of the *Dharma-Kāya*. In that state, birth will be obstructed and Perfect Enlightenment gained.

25 This corresponds to the two stages of *Samādhi* – the visualization stage and the perfected stage.

PART II

The Process of Rebirth

THE CLOSING OF THE DOOR OF THE WOMB
Instructions to the Officiant: again, if through great weakness in devotions and lack of familiarity one be not able to understand, illusion may overcome one, and one will wander to the doors of wombs. The instruction for the closing of the womb-doors becometh very important; call the deceased by name and say this:

O nobly-born, if thou hast not understood the above at this moment, through the influence of *karma*, thou wilt have the impression that thou art either ascending, or moving along on a level, or going downwards. Thereupon, meditate upon the Compassionate One. Remember. Then, as said above, gusts of wind, and icy blasts, hail-storms, and darkness, and impression of being pursued by many people will come upon thee. On fleeing from these [hallucinations], those who are unendowed with meritorious *karma* will have the impression of fleeing into places of misery; those who are endowed with meritorious *karma* will have the impression of arriving in places of happiness. Thereupon, O nobly-born, in whatever continent or place thou art to be born, the signs of that birthplace will shine upon thee then.

For this moment there are several vital profound teachings. Listen undistractedly. Even though thou hast not apprehended by the above settings-face-to-face, here [thou wilt, because] even those who are very weak in devotions will recognize the signs. Therefore listen.

Instructions to the Officiant: now it is very important to employ the methods of closing the womb-door. Wherefore it is necessary to exercise the utmost care. There are two [chief] ways of closing: preventing the being who would enter from entering, and closing the womb-door which might be entered.

METHOD OF PREVENTING ENTRY INTO A WOMB

The instructions for preventing the being from entering are thus:

O nobly-born, (so-and-so by name,) whosoever may have been thy tutelary deity, tranquilly meditate upon him – as upon the reflection of the moon in water, apparent yet non-existent [as a moon], like a magically-produced illusion. If thou hast no special tutelary, meditate either upon the Compassionate Lord or upon me; and, with this in mind, meditate tranquilly.

Then, causing the [visualized form of the] tutelary deity to melt away from the extremities, meditate, without any thought-forming, upon the vacuous Clear Light. This is a very profound art; in virtue of it, a womb is not entered.

THE FIRST METHOD OF CLOSING THE WOMB-DOOR

In that manner meditate; but even though this be found inadequate to prevent thee from entering into a womb, and if thou findest thyself ready to enter into one, then there is the profound teaching for closing the womb-door. Listen thou unto it:

'When, at this time – alas! – the *Sidpa Bardo* is dawning
    upon oneself,
Holding in mind one single resolution,
Persist in joining up the chain of good *karma*;[26]
Close up the womb-door, and remember the opposition.[27]
This is a time when earnestness and pure love are necessary;
Abandon jealousy, and meditate upon the *Guru* Father-Mother.'

Repeat this, from thine own mouth, distinctly; and remember its meaning vividly, and meditate upon it. The putting of this into practice is essential.

The significance of the above teaching, 'When, at this time, the *Sidpa Bardo* is dawning upon me [or upon oneself]', is that now thou art wandering in the *Sidpa Bardo*. As a sign of this, if thou lookest into water, or into mirrors, thou wilt see no reflection of thy face or body; nor doth thy body cast any shadow. Thou hast discarded now thy gross material body of flesh and blood. These are the indications that thou art wandering about in the *Sidpa Bardo*.

At this time, thou must form, without distraction, one single resolve in thy mind. The forming of one single resolve is very important now. It is like directing the course of a horse by the use of the reins.

Whatever thou desirest will come to pass. Think not upon evil actions which might turn the course [of thy mind]. Remember thy [spiritual] relationship with the Reader of this *Bardo Thödol*, or with any one from whom thou hast received teachings, initiation, or spiritual authorization for reading religious texts while in the human world; and persevere in going on with good acts: this is

---

26 The accumulated merit of good actions undertaken on earth by the deceased must be linked to his *Bardo* existence if he is to succeed.

27 'Opposition' here refers to *karmic* propensities, which often lead the deceased in the *Bardo*-plane back towards rebirth – and therefore away from the Perfect Enlightenment of Buddhahood.

very essential. Be not distracted. The boundary line between going upwards or going downwards is here now. If thou givest way to indecision for even a second, thou wilt have to suffer misery for a long, long time. This is the moment. Hold fast to one single purpose. Persistently join up the chain of good acts.

Thou hast come now to the time of closing the womb-door. 'This is a time when earnestness and pure love are necessary', which implieth that now the time hath come when, first of all, the womb-door should be closed, there being five methods of closing. Bear this well at heart.

THE SECOND METHOD OF CLOSING THE WOMB-DOOR

O nobly-born, at this time thou wilt see visions of males and females in union. When thou seest them, remember to withhold thyself from going between them. Regarding the father and mother as thy *Guru* and the Divine Mother, meditate upon them and bow down; humbly exercise thy faith; offer up mental worship with great fervency; and resolve that thou wilt request [of them] religious guidance.

By that resolution alone, the womb ought certainly to be closed; but if it is not closed even by that, and thou findest thyself ready to enter into it, meditate upon the Divine *Guru* Father-Mother, as upon any tutelary deity, or upon the Compassionate Tutelary and Shakti; and meditating upon them, worship them with mental offerings. Resolve earnestly that thou wilt request [of them] a boon. By this, the womb-door ought to be closed.

THE THIRD METHOD OF CLOSING THE WOMB-DOOR

Still, if it be not closed even by that, and thou findest thyself ready to enter the womb, the third method of repelling attachment and repulsion is hereby shown unto thee:

There are four kinds of birth: birth by egg, birth by womb, supernormal birth[28] and birth by heat and moisture.[29] Amongst these four, birth by egg and birth by womb agree in character.

As above said, the visions of males and females in union will appear. If, at that time, one entereth into the womb through the feelings of attachment and repulsion, one may be born either as a horse, a fowl, a dog, or a human being.

If [about] to be born as a male, the feeling of itself being a male dawneth upon the Knower, and a feeling of intense hatred towards the father and of jealousy and attraction towards the mother is begotten. If [about] to be born as a female, the feeling of itself being a female dawneth upon the Knower, and a feeling of intense hatred towards the mother and of intense attraction and fondness towards the father is begotten. Through this secondary cause – [when] entering upon the path of ether, just at the moment when the sperm and the ovum are about to unite – the Knower experienceth the bliss of the simultaneously-born state, during which state it fainteth away into unconsciousness. [Afterwards] it findeth itself encased in oval form, in the embryonic state, and upon emerging from the womb and opening its eyes it may find itself transformed into a young dog. Formerly it had been a human being, but now if it have become a dog it findeth itself undergoing sufferings in a dog's kennel; or [perhaps] as a young pig in a pigsty, or as an ant in an ant-hill, or as an insect, or a grub in a hole, or as a calf, or a kid, or a lamb, from which shape there is no [immediate] returning. Dumbness, stupidity, and miserable intellectual obscurity are suffered, and a variety of sufferings experienced. In like manner, one may wander into hell, or into the world of unhappy ghosts, or throughout the Six *Lokas*, and endure inconceivable miseries.

28 Supernormal birth is the transference of the consciousness-principle from one *loka* (or realm) to another.

29 The process of birth in the vegetable kingdom.

Those who are voraciously inclined towards this [i.e. *sangsāric* existence], or those who do not at heart fear it – O dreadful! O dreadful! Alas! – and those who have not received a *guru's* teachings will fall down into the precipitous depths of the *Sangsāra* in this manner, and suffer interminably and unbearably. Rather than meet with a like fate, listen thou unto my words and bear these teachings of mine at heart.

Reject the feelings of attraction or repulsion, and remember one method of closing the womb-door which I am going to show to thee. Close the womb-door and remember the opposition. This is the time when earnestness and pure love are necessary. As hath been said, 'Abandon jealousy, and meditate upon the *Guru* Father-Mother.'

As above explained, if to be born as a male, attraction towards the mother and repulsion towards the father, and if to be born as a female, attraction towards the father and repulsion towards the mother, together with a feeling of jealousy [for one or the other] which ariseth, will dawn upon thee.

For that time there is a profound teaching. O nobly-born, when the attraction and repulsion arise, meditate as follows:

'Alas! What a being of evil *karma* am I! That I have wandered in the *Sangsāra* hitherto, hath been owing to attraction and repulsion. If I still go on feeling attraction and repulsion, then I shall wander in endless *Sangsāra* and suffer in the Ocean of Misery for a long, long time, by sinking therein. Now I must not act through attraction and repulsion. Alas, for me! Henceforth I will never act through attraction and repulsion.'

Meditating thus, resolve firmly that thou wilt hold on to that [resolution]. It hath been said, in the *Tantras*, 'The door of the womb will be closed up by that alone.'

O nobly-born, be not distracted. Hold thy mind one-pointedly upon that resolution.

THE FOURTH METHOD OF CLOSING THE
WOMB-DOOR

Again, even if that doth not close the womb, and one findeth [oneself] ready to enter the womb, then by means of the teaching [called] 'The Untrue and the Illusory' the womb should be closed. That is to be meditated as follows:

'O, the pair, the father and the mother, the black rain, the storm-blasts, the clashing sounds, the terrifying apparitions, and all the phenomena, are, in their true nature, illusions. Howsoever they may appear, no truth is there [in them]; all substances are unreal and false. Like dreams and like apparitions are they; they are non-permanent; they have no fixity. What advantage is there in being attached [to them]! What advantage is there in having fear and terror of them! It is the seeing of the non-existent as the existent. All these are hallucinations of one's own mind. The illusory mind itself doth not exist from eternity; therefore where should these external [phenomena] exist?

'I, by not having understood these [things] in that way hitherto, have held the non-existent to be the existent, the unreal to be the real, the illusory to be the actual, and have wandered in the *Sangsāra* so long. And even now if I do not recognize them to be illusions, then, wandering in the *Sangsāra* for long ages, [I shall be] certain to fall into the morass of various miseries.

'Indeed, all these are like dreams, like hallucinations, like echoes, like the cities of the Odour-eaters,[30] like mirage, like mirrored forms, like phantasmagoria, like the moon seen in water – not real even for a moment. In truth, they are unreal; they are false.'

By holding one-pointedly to that train of thought, the belief that they are real is dissipated; and, that being impressed upon the inner

---

30 'Odour-eaters' are fairies of Indian and Buddhist mythology who are strongly connected with nature. They can fly through the air, and their cities are clouds which dissolve and disappear in rain.

continuity [of consciousness], one turneth backwards: if the knowledge of the unreality be impressed deeply in that way, the womb-door will be closed.

THE FIFTH METHOD OF CLOSING THE WOMB-DOOR

Still, even when this is done, if the holding [phenomena] as real remaineth undissolved, the womb-door is not closed; and, if one be ready to enter into the womb, thereupon one should close the womb-door by meditating upon the Clear Light, this being the fifth [method]. The meditation is performed as follows:

'Lo! All substances are mine own mind; and this mind is vacuousness, is unborn, and unceasing.'

Thus meditating, allow the mind to rest in the uncreated [state] – like, for example, the pouring of water into water. The mind should be allowed its own easy mental posture, in its natural [or unmodified] condition, clear and vibrant. By maintaining this relaxed, uncreated [state of mind], the womb-doors of the four kinds of birth are sure to be closed. Meditate thus until the closing is successfully accomplished.

Instructions to the Officiant: Many very profound teachings for closing the womb-door have been given above. It is impossible that they should not liberate people of the highest, the average, and the lowest intellectual capacity. If it be asked why this should be so, it is because, firstly, the consciousness in the *Bardo* possessing supernormal power of perception of a limited kind, whatever is spoken to one then is apprehended. Secondly, because – although [formerly] deaf or blind – here, at this time, all one's faculties are perfect, and one can hear whatever is addressed to one. Thirdly, being continually pursued by awe and terror, one thinketh, 'What is best?' and, being alertly conscious, one is always coming to hear whatever may be told to one. Since the consciousness is without a prop, it immediately goeth to whatever place the mind directeth. Fourthly, it is easy to direct it. The memory is ninefold more lucid than before. Even though stupid [before], at this time, by the workings of *karma*, the intellect becometh exceedingly clear and capable of meditating whatever is taught to it. [Hence the answer is], it is because it [i.e. the Knower] possesseth these virtues.

That the performance of funeral rites should be efficacious, is, likewise, because of that reason. Therefore, the perseverance in the reading of the Great *Bardo Thödol* for forty-nine days is of the utmost importance. Even if not liberated at one setting-face-to-face, one ought to be liberated at another; this is why so many different settings-face-to-face are necessary.

THE CHOOSING OF THE WOMB-DOOR

Instructions to the Officiant: There are, nevertheless, many classes of those who – though reminded, and instructed to direct their thoughts one-pointedly – are not liberated, owing to the great force of evil *karmic* obscurations, and because of being unaccustomed to pious deeds, and of being much accustomed to impious deeds throughout the aeons. Therefore, if the womb-door hath not been closed ere this, a teaching also for the selection of a womb-door is going to be given hereinafter. Now, invoking the aid of all the Buddhas and Bodhisattvas, repeat the Refuge; and, once more calling the deceased by name thrice, speak as follows:

O nobly-born, (so-and-so) listen. Although the above setting-face-to-face teachings have been given one-pointedly, yet thou hast not understood them. Therefore, if the womb-door hath not been closed, it is almost time to assume a body. Make thy selection of the womb [according to] this best teaching. Listen attentively, and hold it in mind.

THE PREMONITORY VISIONS OF THE PLACE OF REBIRTH

O nobly-born, now the signs and characteristics of the place of birth will come. Recognize them. In observing the place of birth, choose the continent too.

If to be born in the Eastern Continent of Lüpah, a lake adorned with swans, male and female, [floating thereon], will be seen. Go not there. Recollect the revulsion [against going there]. If one goeth there, [that] Continent – though endowed with bliss and ease – is one wherein religion doth not predominate. Therefore, enter not therein.

If to be born in the Southern Continent of Jambu, grand delightful mansions will be seen. Enter therein, if one is to enter.

If to be born in the Western Continent of Balang-Chöd, a lake adorned with horses, male and female, [grazing on its shores], will be seen. Go not even there, but return here. Although wealth and abundance are there, that being a land wherein religion doth not prevail, enter not therein.

If to be born in the Northern Continent of Daminyan, a lake adorned with male and female cattle [grazing on its shores], or trees [round about it], will be seen. Although duration of life, and merits are there, yet that Continent, too, is one wherein religion doth not predominate. Therefore enter not.

These are the premonitory signs [or visions] of the taking rebirth in those [Continents]. Recognize them. Enter not.

If one is to be born as a *deva*, delightful temples [or mansions] built of various precious metals also will be seen. One may enter therein; so enter therein.

If to be born as an *asura*, either a charming forest will be seen or else circles of fire revolving in opposite directions. Recollect the revulsion; and do not enter therein by any means.

If to be born amongst beasts, rock-caverns and deep holes in the earth and mists will appear. Enter not therein.

If to be born amongst *pretas*, desolate treeless plains and shallow caverns, jungle glades and forest wastes will be seen. If one goeth there, taking birth as a *preta*, one will suffer various pangs of hunger and thirst. Recollect the revulsion; and do not go there by any means. Exert great energy [not to enter therein].

If to be born in Hell, songs [like wailings], due to evil *karma*, will be heard. [One will be] compelled to enter therein unresistingly. Lands of gloom, black houses, and white houses, and black holes in the earth, and black roads along which one hath to go, will appear. If one goeth there, one will enter into Hell; and, suffering unbearable pains of heat and cold, one will be very long in getting out of it.[31] Go not there into the midst of that. It hath been said, 'Exert thine energy to the utmost': this is needed now.

THE PROTECTION AGAINST THE TORMENTING FURIES

O nobly-born, although one liketh it not, nevertheless, being pursued from behind by *karmic* tormenting furies, one feeleth compelled involuntarily to go on; [and with] tormenting furies in the front, and life-cutters as a vanguard leading one, and darkness and *karmic* tornadoes, and noises and snow and rain and terrifying hail-storms and whirlwinds of icy blasts occurring, there will arise the thought of fleeing from them.

Thereupon, by going to seek refuge because of fear, [one beholdeth] the aforesaid visions of great mansions, rock-caverns, earth-caverns, jungles, and lotus blossoms which close [on entering them]; and one escapeth by hiding inside [one of such places] and

---

31 In striking contrast to Christianity, Buddhism offers the chance of eventual escape from hell.

fearing to come out therefrom, and thinking, 'To go out is not good now.' And fearing to depart therefrom, one will feel greatly attracted to one's place of refuge [which is the womb]. Fearful lest, by going out, the awe and terror of the *Bardo* will meet one, and afraid to encounter them, if one hide oneself within [the place or womb chosen], one will thereby assume a very undesirable body and suffer various sufferings.

That [condition] is an indication that evil spirits and *rākṣasas* [or demons] are interfering with one.[32] For this time there is a profound teaching. Listen; and heed it:

At that time – when the tormenting furies will be in pursuit of thee, and when awe and terror will be occurring – instantaneously [visualize] either the Supreme Heruka, or Haya-grīva, or Vajra-Pāni,[33] or [any other] tutelary deity if thou hast such, perfect of form, huge of body, of massive limbs, wrathful and terrifying in appearance, capable of reducing to dust all mischievous spirits. Visualize it instantaneously. The gift-waves and the power of its grace will separate thee from the tormenting furies and thou wilt obtain the power to select the womb-door. This is the vital art of the very profound teaching; therefore bear it thoroughly well in mind.

O nobly-born, the *dhyānī* and other deities are born of the power of *Samādhi* [or meditation]. *Pretas* [or unhappy spirits or shades] and malignant spirits of certain orders are those who by changing their feeling [or mental attitude] while in the Intermediate State assumed that very shape which they thereafter retained, and became *pretas*, evil spirits, and *rākṣasas*, possessed of the power of shape-shifting. All *pretas*, who exist in space, who traverse the sky, and the eighty thousand species of mischievous sprites, have become

---

32 Preventing one from achieving a good rebirth – or, indeed, rebirth at all.

33 These three deities are all believed to be particularly powerful at purging a person of evil spirits.

so by changing their feelings [while] in the mental-body [on the *Bardo*-plane].[34]

At this time, if one can recollect the Great Symbol [teachings] concerning the Voidness, that will be best. If one be not trained in that, train the [mental] powers into [regarding] all things as illusion [or *māyā*]. Even if this be impossible, be not attracted by anything. By meditating upon the Tutelary Deity, the Great Compassionate [One], Buddhahood will be obtained in the *Sambhoga-Kāya*.

THE ALTERNATIVE CHOOSING: SUPERNORMAL BIRTH; OR WOMB-BIRTH

If, however, O nobly-born, thou hast, because of the influence of *karma*, to enter into a womb, the teaching for the selection of the womb-door will be explained now. Listen.

Do not enter into any sort of womb which may be come by. If compelled by tormenting furies to enter, meditate upon Hayagriva.

Since thou now possesseth a slender supernormal power of foreknowledge, all the places [of birth] will be known to thee, one after another.[35] Choose accordingly.

There are two alternatives: the transference [of the conscious-ness-principle] to a pure Buddha realm, and the selection of the impure *sangsāric* womb-door, to be accomplished as follows:

---

34 All of these dwellers in the *Bardo*-plane (*pretas*, evil spirits, *rākṣhasas*, sprites, and, some-times, deceased human beings) hold the false belief that it is a desirable or fixed state of existence, so their normal progress has been delayed. A *Bardo*-bound spirit may remain in such a state from five hundred to a thousand years. In exceptional cases the time might stretch to ages. The deceased is in flux, unable either to advance to a paradise realm or be reborn in the human world. Ultimately, however, a womb will be entered and *Bardo* exist-ence will draw to a close.

35 Informed by visions, the Knower will become aware of the destiny of each womb.

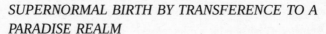

SUPERNORMAL BIRTH BY TRANSFERENCE TO A PARADISE REALM

In the first – the transference to a pure paradise – the projection is directed [by thinking or meditating] thus:

> 'Alas! How sorrowful it is that I, during all the innumerable *kalpas* since illimitable, beginningless time, until now, have been wandering in the Quagmire of *Sangsāra*! O how painful that I have not been liberated into Buddhahood by knowing the consciousness to be the self hitherto ere this! Now doth this *Sangsāra* disgust me, horrify me, sicken me; now hath the hour come to prepare to flee from it. I myself will so act as to be born in The Happy Western Realm, at the feet of the Buddha Amitābha,[36] miraculously from amidst a lotus blossom.'

Thinking thus, direct the resolution [or wish] earnestly [to that Realm]; or, likewise, to any Realm thou mayst desire – The Pre-eminently Happy Realm, or The Thickly-Formed Realm, or The Realm [of Those] of Long Hair,[37] or the Illimitable Vihāra of the Lotus Radiance,[38] in Urgyan's presence; or direct thy wish to any Realm which thou desirest most, in undistracted one-pointedness [of mind]. By doing so, birth will take place in that Realm instantaneously.

Or, if thou desirest to go to the presence of Maitreya, in the Tuṣhita Heavens, by directing an earnest wish in like manner and thinking, 'I will go to the presence of Maitreya in the Tuṣhita

---

36 Literally 'The Buddha of Infinite Light', Buddha Amitābha is a divine power inherent in The Happy Western Realm.

37 The Paradise of Vajra-Pāni, which is not a Buddha realm.

38 The realm reigned over by Great *Guru* Padma Sambhava (or Urgyan).

Heavens,[39] for the hour hath struck for me here in the Intermediate State,' birth will be obtained miraculously inside a lotus blossom in the presence of Maitreya.

WOMB-BIRTH: THE RETURN TO THE HUMAN WORLD

If, however, such [a supernormal birth] be not possible, and one delighteth in entering a womb or hath to enter, there is a teaching for the selection of the womb-door of impure *Sangsāra*. Listen:

Looking with thy supernormal power of foresight over the Continents, as above, choose that in which religion prevaileth and enter therein.

If birth is to be obtained over a heap of impurities, a sensation that it is sweet-smelling will attract one towards that impure mass, and birth will be obtained thereby.

Whatsoever they [the wombs or visions] may appear to be, do not regard them as they are [or seem]; and by not being attracted or repelled a good womb should be chosen. In this, too, since it is important to direct the wish, direct it thus:

'Ah! I ought to take birth as a Universal Emperor; or as a Brāhmin, like a great sal-tree;[40] or as the son of an adept in *siddhic* powers; or in a spotless hierarchical line; or in the caste of a man who is filled with [religious] faith; and, being born so, be endowed with great merit so as to be able to serve all sentient beings.'

Thinking thus, direct thy wish, and enter into the womb. At the same time, emit thy gift-waves [of grace, or good-will] upon the womb which thou art entering, [transforming it thereby] into a

39 Birth from a lotus blossom in the Tuṣhita Heavens implies purity: that is, a womb, which is considered impure, is not involved. It recalls the traditional belief that Padmasambhava was born of a lotus flower.

40 For Buddhists the sal-tree is sanctified by the fact that the birth and death of the first Buddha took place beneath such a tree.

celestial mansion. And believing that the Conquerors and their Sons [or Bodhisattvas] of the Ten Directions,[41] and the tutelary deities, especially the Great Compassionate [One], are conferring power thereon, pray unto Them, and enter the womb.

In selecting the womb-door thus, there is a possibility of error: through the influence of *karma*, good wombs may appear bad and bad wombs may appear good; such error is possible. At that time, too, the art of the teaching being important, thereupon do as follows:

Even though a womb may appear good, do not be attracted; if it appear bad, have no repulsion towards it. To be free from repulsion and attraction, or from the wish to take or to avoid – to enter in the mood of complete impartiality – is the most profound of arts. Excepting only for the few who have had some practical experience [in psychical development], it is difficult to get rid of the remnants of the disease of evil propensities.

Instructions to the Officiant: Therefore, if unable to part with the attraction and repulsion, those of the least mentality and of evil *karma* will be liable to take refuge amongst brutes. The way to repel therefrom is to call the deceased by name again, thus:

O nobly-born, if thou art not able to rid thyself of attraction and repulsion, and know not the [art of] selecting the womb-door, whichever of the above visions may appear, call upon the Precious Trinity and take refuge [therein].

Pray unto the Great Compassionate One. Walk with thy head erect. Know thyself in the *Bardo*. Cast away all weakness and attraction towards thy sons and daughters or any relations left behind thee; they can be of no use to thee. Enter upon the White Light-[Path] of the *devas*, or upon the Yellow Light-[Path] of human beings; enter into the great mansions of precious metals and into the delightful gardens.

41 These ten are: the four cardinal points, the four midway points, the nadir and the zenith.

Instructions to the Officiant: Repeat that [address to the deceased] seven times over.

Then there should be offered 'The Invocation of the Buddhas and Bodhisattvas'; 'The Path of Good Wishes Giving Protection from Fears in the *Bardo*'; 'The Root Words [or Verses] of the *Bardo*'; and 'The Rescuer [or Path of Good Wishes for Saving] from the Ambuscades [or Dangerous Narrow Passage-Way] of the *Bardo*'. These are to be read over thrice. 'The *Tahdol*', which liberateth the body-aggregate,[42] should also be read out. Then 'The Rite which Conferreth of Itself Liberation in [Virtue of] Propensity'[43] should be read too.

THE GENERAL CONCLUSION

By the reading of these properly, those devotees [or *yogis*] who are advanced in understanding can make the best use of the Transference at the moment of death. They need not traverse the Intermediate State, but will depart by the Great Straight-Upward [Path]. Others who are a little less practised [in things spiritual], recognizing the Clear Light in the *Chönyid Bardo*, at the moment of death, will go by the upward [course]. Those lower than these will be liberated – in accordance with their particular abilities and *karmic* connections – when one or other of the Peaceful and Wrathful Deities dawneth upon them, during the succeeding [two] weeks, while in the *Chönyid Bardo*.

There being several turning-points, liberation should be obtained at one or other of them through recognizing. But those of very weak *karmic* connections, whose mass of obscuration is great

42 According to some Tibetan systems of *yoga*, the aggregate of the human body comprises twenty-seven parts, including the five elements, the five sense organs, and the mentality. Together, these parts make up the transient human personality.

43 A shorter, metrical version of the *Bardo Thödol*, which is easy to recite and memorize. It is thought that, by knowing the ritual by heart, liberation from the *Bardo*-plane will come more easily to the deceased.

[because of] evil actions, have to wander downwards and down-wards to the *Sidpa Bardo*. Yet since there are, like the rungs of a ladder, many kinds of settings-face-to-face [or reminders], liber-ation should have been obtained at one or at another by recognizing. But those of the weakest *karmic* connections, by not recognizing, fall under the influence of awe and terror. [For them] there are various graded teachings for closing the womb-door and for selecting the womb-door; and, at one or other of these, they should have apprehended the method of visualization and [applied] the illimitable virtues [thereof] for exalting one's own condition. Even the lowest of them, resembling the brute order, will have been able – in virtue of the application of the Refuge – to turn from entering into misery; and, [obtaining] the great [boon] of a perfectly endowed and freed human body,[44] will, in the next birth, meeting with a guru who is a virtuous friend, obtain the [saving] vows.

If this Doctrine arrive [while one is] in the *Sidpa Bardo*, it will be like the connecting up of good actions, resembling [thus] the placing of a trough in [the break of] a broken drain; such is this Teaching.

Those of heavy evil *karma* cannot possibly fail to be liberated by hearing this Doctrine [and recognizing]. If it be asked, why? It is because, at that time, all the Peaceful and Wrathful Deities being present to receive [one], and the *Māras* and the Interrupters likewise coming to receive [one] along with them, the mere hearing of this Doctrine then turneth one's views, and liberation is obtained; for there is no flesh and blood body to depend upon, but a mental body, which is [easily] affected. At whatever distance one may be

---

44 That is, 'freed' from the eight thraldoms: the ever-recurring round of pleasure of the *deva*; the perpetual conflict of the *asura*; the unavoidable drudgery associated with existence in worlds such as that of the brutes; the anguish of hunger and thirst of the *preta*; the extremes of heat and cold for dwellers in Hell; the atheism or deviant religion among some of the races of mankind; the physical limitations associated with certain human births; and other hindrances associated with certain human births.

wandering in the *Bardo*, one heareth and cometh, for one possesseth the slender sense of supernormal perception and foreknowledge; and, recollecting and apprehending instantaneously, the mind is capable of being changed [or influenced]. Therefore is it [i.e. the Teaching] of great use here. It is like the mechanism of a catapult. It is like the moving of a big wooden beam [or log] which a hundred men cannot carry, but which by being floated upon water can be towed wherever desired in a moment. It is like the controlling of a horse's mouth by means of a bridle.

Therefore, going near [the body of] one who hath passed out of this life – if the body be there – impress this [upon the spirit of the deceased] vividly, again and again, until blood and the yellowish water-secretion begin to issue from the nostrils. At that time the corpse should not be disturbed. The rules to be observed for this [impressing to be efficacious] are: no animal should be slain on account of the deceased;[45] nor should relatives weep or make mournful wailings near the dead body;[46] [let the family] perform virtuous deeds as far as possible.

In other ways, too, this Great Doctrine of the *Bardo Thödol*, as well as any other religious texts, may be expounded [to the dead or dying]. If this [Doctrine] be joined to the end of *The Guide* and recited [along with *The Guide*] it becometh very efficacious. In yet other ways it should be recited as often as possible. The words and meanings should be committed to memory [by everyone]; and, when death is inevitable and the death-symptoms are recognized – strength permitting – one should recite it oneself, and reflect upon the meanings. If strength doth not permit, then a friend should read the Book and impress it vividly. There is no doubt as to its liberating.

---

45 This rule does not refer to the sacrifice of animals on behalf of the deceased, but to the practice, against Buddhist beliefs, of killing animals in order to provide food for the *lāmas* and the guests at the funeral.

46 Buddhism discourages such displays of grief.

The Doctrine is one which liberateth by being seen, without need of meditation or of *sādhanā*;[47] this Profound Teaching liberateth by being heard or by being seen. This Profound Teaching liberateth those of great evil *karma* through the Secret Pathway. One should not forget its meaning and the words, even though pursued by seven mastiffs.

By this Select Teaching, one obtaineth Buddhahood at the moment of death. Were the Buddhas of the Three Times [the Past, the Present, and the Future] to seek, They could not find any doctrine transcending this.

Thus is completed the Profound Heart-Drops of the *Bardo* Doctrine, called the *Bardo Thödol*, which liberateth embodied beings.

[Here endeth *The Tibetan Book of the Dead*]

47 Literally 'perfect devotion' – an intricate and technically perfect ritual.

THE APPENDIX

In our Manuscript (but not in the Block-Print), directly following the text of the *Bardo Thödol*, there are thirteen folios of rituals and prayers (lit., 'paths of good wishes'), which all professional readers of the *Bardo Thödol* must know, usually from memory, and apply as needed; and they are here rendered into English as follows:

I: THE INVOCATION OF THE BUDDHAS AND BODHISATTVAS

Instructions to the Officiant: The invoking of the Buddhas and Bodhisattvas for assistance, when [any one is] dying, is [thus]:

Offer up to the Trinity whatever actual offerings can be offered [by the dying person, or by his family], together with mentally-created offerings: and, holding in the hand sweet-smelling incense, repeat, with great fervency, the following:

> O ye Buddhas and Bodhisattvas, abiding in the Ten
> Directions, endowed with great compassion,
> endowed with foreknowledge, endowed with the
> divine eye, endowed with love, affording protec-
> tion to sentient beings, condescend through the
> power of your great compassion to come hither;

condescend to accept these offerings actually laid out and mentally created.

O ye Compassionate Ones, ye possess the wisdom of understanding, the love of compassion, the power of [doing] divine deeds and of protecting, in incomprehensible measure. Ye Compassionate Ones (such-and-such a person) is passing from this world to the world beyond. He is leaving this world. He is taking a great leap. No friends [hath he]. Misery is great. [He is without] defenders, without protectors, without forces and kinsmen. The light of this world hath set. He goeth to another place. He entereth thick darkness. He falleth down a steep precipice. He entereth into a jungle solitude. He is pursued by *Karmic* Forces. He goeth into the Vast Silence. He is borne away by the Great Ocean. He is wafted on the Wind of *Karma*. He goeth in the direction where stability existeth not. He is caught by the Great Conflict. He is obsessed by the Great Afflicting Spirit. He is awed and terrified by the Messengers of the Lord of Death. Existing *Karma* putteth him into repeated existence. No strength hath he. He hath come upon a time when he hath to go alone.

O ye Compassionate Ones, defend (so-and-so) who is defenceless. Protect him who is unprotected. Be his forces and his kinsmen. Protect [him] from the great gloom of the *Bardo*. Turn him from the red [or storm] wind of *Karma*. Turn him from the great awe and terror of the Lords of Death. Save him from the long narrow passage-way of the *Bardo*.

O ye Compassionate Ones, let not the force of your compassion be weak; but aid him. Let him not go into misery [or the miserable states of existence]. Forget not your ancient vows; and let not the force of your compassion be weak.

O ye Buddhas and Bodhisattvas, let not the might of the method of your compassion be weak towards this one. Catch hold of him with [the hook of] your grace. Let not the sentient being fall under the power of evil *karma*.

O ye Trinity, protect him from the miseries of the *Bardo*. Saying this with great humility and faith, let thyself and [all] others [present] repeat it thrice.

II: 'THE PATH OF GOOD WISHES FOR SAVING FROM THE DANGEROUS NARROW PASSAGEWAY OF THE BARDO' IS [AS FOLLOWS]:

[1]

O ye Conquerors and your Sons, abiding in the Ten
    Directions,
O ye ocean-like Congregation of the All-Good Conquerors,
    the Peaceful and the Wrathful,
O ye *Gurus* and *Devas*, and ye *Ḍākinīs*, the Faithful Ones,
Hearken now out of [your] great love and compassion:
Obeisance, O ye assemblage of *Gurus* and *Ḍākinīs*;
Out of your great love, lead us along the Path.

[2]

When, through illusion, I and others are wandering in the
    Sangsāra,
Along the bright light-path of undistracted listening, reflec-
    tion, and meditation,
May the *Gurus* of the Inspired Line lead us,
May the bands of Mothers be our rear-guard,
May we be saved from the fearful narrow passage-way of
    the *Bardo*,
May we be placed in the state of the perfect Buddhahood.

[3]

When, through violent anger, [we are] wandering in the *Sangsāra*,
Along the bright light-path of the Mirror-like Wisdom,
May the Bhagavān Vajra-Sattva lead us,
May the Mother Māmakī be our rear-guard,
May we be saved from the fearful narrow passage-way of
    the *Bardo*,
May we be placed in the state of the perfect Buddhahood.

[4]

When, through intense pride, [we are] wandering in the *Sangsāra*,
Along the bright light-path of the Wisdom of Equality,
May the Bhagavān Ratna-Sambhava lead us,
May the Mother, She-of-the-Buddha-Eye, be our rear-guard,
May we be saved from the fearful narrow passage-way of
    the *Bardo*,
May we be placed in the state of the perfect Buddhahood.

[5]

When, through great attachment, [we are] wandering in the
    Sangsāra,
Along the bright light-path of the Discriminating Wisdom,
May the Bhagavān Amitābha lead us,
May the Mother, [She]-of-White-Raiment, be our rear-guard,
May we be saved from the fearful narrow passage-way of
    the *Bardo*,
May we be placed in the state of the perfect Buddhahood.

[6]

When, through intense jealousy, [we are] wandering in the
    Sangsāra,
Along the bright light-path of the All-Performing Wisdom,

May the Bhagavān Amogha-Siddhi lead us,

May the Mother, the Faithful Tārā, be our rear-guard,

May we be saved from the fearful narrow passage-way of the *Bardo*,

May we be placed in the state of the perfect Buddhahood.

[7]

When, through intense stupidity, [we are] wandering in the *Sangsāra*,

Along the bright light-path of the Wisdom of Reality,

May the Bhagavān Vairochana lead us,

May the Mother of Great Space be our rear-guard,

May we be saved from the fearful narrow passage-way of the *Bardo*,

May we be placed in the state of the perfect Buddhahood.

[8]

When, through intense illusion, [we are] wandering in the *Sangsāra*,

Along the bright light-path of the abandonment of hallucinatory fear, awe, and terror,

May the bands of the Bhagavāns of the Wrathful Ones lead us,

May the bands of the Wrathful Goddesses Rich-in-Space be our rear-guard,

May we be saved from the fearful narrow passage-way of the *Bardo*,

May we be placed in the state of the perfect Buddhahood.

[9]

When, through intense propensities, [we are] wandering in the *Sangsāra*,

Along the bright light-path of the Simultaneously-born
Wisdom,

May the heroic Knowledge-Holders lead us,

May the bands of the Mothers, the *Ḍākinīs*, be our rear-
guard,

May we be saved from the fearful narrow passage-way of
the *Bardo*,

May we be placed in the state of the perfect Buddhahood.

[10]

May the ethereal elements not rise up as enemies;

May it come that we shall see the Realm of the Blue Buddha.

May the watery elements not rise up as enemies;

May it come that we shall see the Realm of the White Buddha.

May the earthy elements not rise up as enemies;

May it come that we shall see the Realm of the Yellow
Buddha.

May the fiery elements not rise up as enemies;

May it come that we shall see the Realm of the Red Buddha.

May the airy elements not rise up as enemies;

May it come that we shall see the Realm of the Green Buddha.[1]

May the elements of the rainbow colours not rise up as
enemies;

May it come that all the Realms of the Buddhas will be seen.

May it come that all the Sounds [in the Bardo] will be known
as one's own sounds;

May it come that all the Radiances will be known as one's
own radiances;

May it come that the *Tri-Kāya* will be realized in the *Bardo*.

---

1 The Blue Buddha is Samanta-Bhadra; the White Buddha is Vajra-Sattva; the Yellow Buddha
is Ratna-Sambhava; the Red Buddha is Amitābha; and the Green Buddha is Amogha-Siddhi.

III: HERE BEGINNETH *'THE ROOT VERSES OF THE SIX BARDOS'*

[1]

O now, when the Birthplace *Bardo* upon me is dawning!

Abandoning idleness – there being no idleness in [a devotee's] life –

Entering into the Reality undistractedly, listening, reflecting, and meditating,

Carrying on to the Path [knowledge of the true nature of] appearances and of mind, may the *Tri-Kāya* be realized:

Once that the human form hath been attained,

May there be no time [or opportunity] in which to idle it [or human life] away.

[2]

O now, when the Dream *Bardo* upon me is dawning!

Abandoning the inordinate corpse-like sleeping of the sleep of stupidity,

May the consciousness undistractedly be kept in its natural state;

Grasping the [true nature of] dreams, [may I] train [myself] in the Clear Light of Miraculous Transformation:

Acting not like the brutes in slothfulness,

May the blending of the practising of the sleep [state] and actual [or waking] experience be highly valued [by me].

[3]

O now, when the *Dhyāna Bardo* upon me is dawning!

Abandoning the whole mass of distractions and illusions,

May [the mind] be kept in the mood of endless undistracted *Samādhi*,

May firmness both in the visualizing and in the perfected [stages] be obtained:

At this time, when meditating one-pointedly, with [all other] actions put aside,

May I not fall under the power of misleading, stupefying passions.

[4]

O now, when the *Bardo* of the Moment of Death upon me is dawning!

Abandoning attraction and craving, and weakness for all [worldly things],

May I be undistracted in the space of the bright [enlightening] teachings,

May I [be able to] transfuse myself into the heavenly space of the Unborn:

The hour hath come to part with this body composed of flesh and blood;

May I know the body to be impermanent and illusory.

[5]

O now, when the *Bardo* of the Reality upon me is dawning,

Abandoning all awe, fear, and terror of all [phenomena],

May I recognize whatever appeareth as being mine own thought-forms,

May I know them to be apparitions in the Intermediate State;

[It hath been said], 'There arriveth a time when the chief turning-point is reached;

Fear not the bands of the Peaceful and Wrathful, Who are thine own thought-forms.'

[6]

O now, when the *Bardo* of [taking] Rebirth upon me is dawning!

One-pointedly holding fast to a single wish,

[May I be able to] continue the course of good deeds through
   repeated efforts;

May the womb-door be closed and the revulsion recollected:

The hour hath come when energy and pure love are needed;

[May I] cast off jealousy and meditate upon the *Guru*, the
   Father-Mother.

[7]

['O] procrastinating one, who thinketh not of the coming of
   death,

Devoting thyself to the useless doings of this life,

Improvident art thou in dissipating thy great opportunity;

Mistaken, indeed, will thy purpose be now if thou returnest
   empty-handed [from this life]:

Since the Holy Dharma is known to be thy true need,

Wilt thou not devote [thyself] to the Holy Dharma even now?'

EPILOGUE

Thus say the Great Adepts in devotion.

If the chosen teaching of the *guru* be not borne in mind,

Wilt thou not [O *shishya*] be acting even as a traitor to
   thyself?

It is of great importance that these Root Words be known.

IV: HERE BEGINNETH 'THE PATH OF GOOD WISHES WHICH PROTECTETH FROM FEAR IN THE BARDO'

[1]

When the cast [of the dice] of my life hath become exhausted,

The relatives in this world avail me not;

When I wander alone by myself in the *Bardo*,

[O] ye Conquerors, Peaceful and Wrathful, exercising the
power of your compassion,

Let it come that the Gloom of Ignorance be dispelled.

[2]

When wandering alone, parted from loving friends,

When the shapes of mine empty thought-forms dawn upon
me here,

[May the] Buddhas, exerting the power of their divine
compassion,

Cause it to come that there be neither awe nor terror in the
Bardo.

[3]

When the bright radiances of the Five Wisdoms shine upon
me now,

Let it come that I, neither awed nor terrified, may recognize
them to be of myself;

When the apparitions of the Peaceful and Wrathful forms
are dawning upon me here,

Let it come that I, obtaining the assurance of fearlessness,
may recognize the *Bardo*.

[4]

When experiencing miseries, because of the force of evil *karma*,

Let it come that the Conquerors, the Peaceful and Wrathful,
may dispel the miseries;

When the self-existing Sound of Reality reverberates [like]
a thousand thunders,

Let it come that they be transmuted into the sounds of the
Mahāyāna Doctrines.

[5]

When [I am] unprotected, [and] *karmic* influences have to
be followed here,

I beseech the Conquerors, the Peaceful and the Wrathful, to
protect me;

When suffering miseries, because of the *karmic* influence
of propensities,

Let it come that the blissful *Samādhi* of the Clear Light may
dawn [upon me].

[6]

When assuming supernormal rebirth in the *Sidpa Bardo*,

Let it come that the perverting revelations of *Māra* occur
not therein;

When I arrive wheresoever I wish to,

Let it come that I experience not the illusory fright and awe
from evil *karma*.

[7]

When the roarings of savage beasts are uttered,

Let it come that they be changed into the sacred sounds of
the Six Syllables;

When pursued by snow, rain, wind, and darkness,

Let it come that I see with the celestial eyes of bright
Wisdom.

[8]

Let it come that all sentient beings of the same harmonious
order in the *Bardo*,

Without jealousy [towards one another], obtain birth on the
higher planes;

When [destined to] suffering from intense miseries of hunger
and thirst,[2]

Let it come that I experience not the pangs of hunger and
thirst, heat and cold.

[9]

When I behold the future parents in union,

Let it come that I behold them as the [Divine] Pair, the
Conquerors, the Peaceful and the Wrathful Father and
Mother;

Obtaining the power of being born anywhere, for the good
of others,

Let it come that I obtain the perfect body, adorned with the
signs and the graces.[3]

[10]

Obtaining for myself the body of a male [which is] the better,

Let it come that I liberate all who see or hear me;

Allowing not the evil *karma* to follow me,

Let it come that whatever merits [be mine] follow me and
be multiplied.

[11]

Wherever I be born, there and then,

Let it come that I meet the Conquerors, the Peaceful and
the Wrathful Deities;

Being able to walk and to talk as soon as [I am] born,[4]

---

2   'Hunger and thirst' refers to the sufferings of the *preta* in the *Bardo*-plane; 'heat and cold'
    refers to an existence in Hell.

3   That is, the body of a Buddha, with its supernormal attributes and powers.

4   At birth, the Buddha is said to have taken seven steps forward and proclaimed a divine
    statement. At each step a lotus flower, the symbol of Enlightenment, appeared on the ground.
    The baby's seven steps also evoke seven directions: four cardinal, plus up, down and here.

Let it come that I obtain the non-forgetting intellect and remember my past life [or lives].

[12]

In all the various lores, great, small, and intermediate,

Let it come that I be able to obtain mastery merely upon hearing, reflecting, and seeing;

In whatever place I be born, let it be auspicious;

Let it come that all sentient beings be endowed with happiness.

[13]

Ye Conquerors, Peaceful and Wrathful, in likeness to your bodies,

[Number of your] followers, duration of your life-period, limit of your realms,

And [in likeness to the] goodness of your divine name,

Let it come that I, and others, equal your very selves in all these.

[14]

By the divine grace of the innumerable All-Good Peaceful and Wrathful [Ones],

And by the gift-waves of the wholly pure Reality,

[And] by the gift-waves of the one-pointed devotion of the mystic devotees,

Let it come that whatsoever be wished for be fulfilled here and now.

'The Path of Good Wishes which Protecteth from Fear in the *Bardo*' is finished.

V: THE COLOPHON

The Manuscript concludes with the following seven verses by the
lāma or scribe who compiled it, but he – faithful to the old *lāmaic*
teaching that the human personality should be self-abased and the
Scriptures alone exalted before the gaze of the sentient creatures
– has not recorded his name:

Through the perfectly pure intention of mine
In the making of this, through the root of the merits thereof,
[May] those protectorless sentient beings, Mothers,
[Be] placed in the State of the Buddha:
Let the radiant glory of auspiciousness come to illuminate
    the world;
Let this Book be auspicious;
Let virtue and goodness be perfected in every way.

[Here endeth the Manuscript of the *Bardo Thödol*.]